I0123757

War, Peace, and Populist Discourse in Ukraine

This book explores the detrimental effects on global peace of populism's tendency to present complex social issues in simplistic "good versus evil" terms. Analyzing the civilizational discourse of Ukrainian President Volodymyr Zelensky with respect to the ongoing war between Russia and Ukraine—with his division of the world into "civilized us" versus "barbarian them"—the book argues that such a one-dimensional representation of complex social reality leaves no space for understanding the conflict and has little, if any, potential to bring about peace.

To deconstruct the "civilization versus barbarism" discourse propagated by Zelensky, the book incorporates into its analysis alternative articulations of the crisis by oppositional voices. The author looks at the writing of several popular Ukrainian journalists and bloggers who have been excluded from the field of political representation within Ukraine, where all oppositional media are currently banned. Drawing on the discourse theory of Ernesto Laclau and Chantal Mouffe, the author argues that the incorporation of alternative perspectives, and silenced voices, is vitally important for understanding the complexity of all international conflicts, including the current one between Russia and Ukraine.

This timely and important study will be relevant for all students and scholars of media and communication studies, populist rhetoric, political communication, journalism, area studies, international relations, linguistics, discourse analysis, propaganda, and peace studies.

Olga Baysha is Associate Professor in Media and Communication at the National Research University "Higher School of Economics," Moscow, Russia. She earned her MS in Journalism from Colorado State University and PhD in Communication from the University of Colorado Boulder. Previously, she worked as a news reporter and editor in Kharkiv and Kyiv, Ukraine. She is the author of *The Mythologies of Capitalism and the End of the Soviet Project* (2014), *Miscommunicating Social Change: Lessons from Russia and Ukraine* (2018), and *Democracy, Populism, and Neoliberalism in Ukraine: On the Fringes of the Virtual and the Real* (2022).

Routledge Focus on Communication Studies

Globalism and Gendering Cancer
Tracking the Trope of Oncogenic Women from the US to Kenya
Miriam O'Kane Mara

Maatian Ethics in a Communication Context
Melba Vélez Ortiz

Enhancing Intercultural Communication in Organizations
Insights From Project Advisers
Edited by Roos Beerkens, Emmanuelle Le Pichon, Roselinde Supheert, Jan D. ten Thije

Communicating Aggression in a Megamedia World
Beata Sierocka

Multigenerational Communication in Organizations
Insights from the Workplace
Michael G. Strawser, Stephanie A. Smith and Bridget Rubenking

Participatory Community Inquiry in the Opioid Epidemic
A New Approach for Communities in Crisis
Craig Maier

Democracy, Populism, and Neoliberalism in Ukraine
On the Fringes of the Virtual and the Real
Olga Baysha

War, Peace and Populist Discourse in Ukraine
Olga Baysha

For more information about this series, please visit: www.routledge.com

War, Peace, and Populist Discourse in Ukraine

Olga Baysha

Routledge
Taylor & Francis Group

NEW YORK AND LONDON

First published 2023
by Routledge
605 Third Avenue, New York, NY 10158

and by Routledge
4 Park Square, Milton Park, Abingdon, Oxon OX14 4RN

Routledge is an imprint of the Taylor & Francis Group, an informa business

© 2023 Olga Baysha

British Library Cataloguing-in-Publication Data
A catalogue record for this book is available from the British Library

Library of Congress Cataloging-in-Publication Data
Names: Baysha, Olga, author.
Title: War, peace, and populist discourse in Ukraine / Olga Baysha.
Description: New York, NY : Routledge, 2024. | Series: Routledge
   focus in communication studies | Includes bibliographical references
   and index.
Identifiers: LCCN 2023012788 (print) | LCCN 2023012789 (ebook) |
   ISBN 9781032455358 (hardback) | ISBN 9781032458922
   (paperback) | ISBN 9781003379164 (ebook)
Subjects: LCSH: Communication in politics—Ukraine. | Populism—
   Ukraine. | Ukraine—History—Russian Invasion, 2022—Press
   coverage. | Ukraine—Politics and government—20th century. |
   Zelensky, Volodymyr, 1978—Political and social views.
Classification: LCC JA85.2.U38 B39 2024 (print) | LCC JA85.2.U38
   (ebook) | DDC 320.56/62094770904—dc23/eng/20230419
LC record available at https://lccn.loc.gov/2023012788
LC ebook record available at https://lccn.loc.gov/2023012789

ISBN: 978-1-032-45535-8 (hbk)
ISBN: 978-1-032-45892-2 (pbk)
ISBN: 978-1-003-37916-4 (ebk)

DOI: 10.4324/9781003379164

Typeset in Times New Roman
by Apex CoVantage, LLC

To all my dear people in Ukraine

Contents

Acknowledgments

I am forever grateful to all my colleagues and friends supporting me through these difficult times: Leah and Oliver Boyd-Barrett, Irina Puchkova, Natalia Semenikhina, Elena Murzina, Elena Romanova, Natalia Knoblock, Janice Peck, Marco Briziarelli, Ilya Kiria, Konstantin Kevorkyan, Lilia and Oleg Pukhnavtsev, Hlib Baisha, and many others.

I am also very thankful for my research assistants, Sabina Balishyan and Kamilla Chukasheva. Thank you for your diligence—your help was priceless.

As usual, my special thanks go to Justin Maki, whose proofreading and editing make my ideas more readable. Thank you so much for your time, professionalism, and enduring willingness to help.

Acknowledgments

Introduction

Transnational Populism and Global Polarization

When Populism Goes Abroad

Traditionally, populism has been considered a phenomenon of domestic politics. The Manichean division of the social into two irreconcilable parts, "good people" versus "bad elites"—the main feature of populism (Mudde & Kaltwasser, 2017)—has usually been performed within the context of individual nation-states. However, because the boundary separating the domestic from the foreign has become increasingly blurred, with many domestic issues gaining international dimensions and many international developments affecting domestic affairs, at least some types of populism have acquired a transnational orientation. As most of the problems that affect people's lives in our interconnected world—migration, terrorism, pandemics, and so on—do not respect national borders, populists must take the transboundary character of these challenges into consideration when working out their responses.

This trend has only been facilitated by rapid real-time communication, which increases the interconnectedness of the world and people's awareness of the global dimensions of their problems. Reflecting on these developments, a growing number of academic studies, which draw on various theoretical traditions and analyze different sociopolitical milieus, address the influence of present-day populism on international relations, including on foreign policy and security decisions (e.g., Chryssogelos, 2020; De Cleen et al., 2020; De la Torre, 2018; Destradi & Plagemann, 2019; Grzymala-Busse, 2019; Hadiz & Chryssogelos, 2017; Moffitt, 2017).

The growing recognition that current populism has transcended national borders makes it more difficult to accept that populist policies are necessarily anti-cosmopolitan, inward-oriented, and concerned with fighting exclusively against domestic "enemies of the people," as the traditional view of populism would suggest (Müller, 2017). Instead, there is a widely shared belief that the "populist explosion" (Judis, 2016) of the past decade came about as a reaction to the inequalities and injustices of the global neoliberal order, which has made national governments less powerful in terms of providing security to their citizens and thereby led to a radical increase of social inequality on

DOI: 10.4324/9781003379164-1

the global stage (Fraser, 2019; Harvey, 2018; Žižek, 2018). Presented this way, the populist explosion appears to be a backlash against globalization, the increasing influence of "international bureaucracies," and/or resentment regarding Westernization within non-Western contexts. In this view, therefore, populism is seen as a riposte to "liberal internationalism" (Jahn, 2018, p. 44), which—as has been broadly assumed—naturally leads populists to demonize globalism and its agents.

Conventional populist resentments toward global institutions of power are not only about portraying state bureaucracies as the servants of foreign interests but also about the lack of transparency in their decision-making processes (Voeten, 2020). Populists accuse bureaucrats in charge of regional and global governance of implementing ostensibly democratic procedures in corrupt ways that put globalists beyond any accountability to the people's will. Against such corrupted agents of globalization, populists portray themselves as belonging to the people and serving as their genuine representatives (Biegon, 2019). Because of this, for many scholars of populism, a basic antagonism "between national sovereignty, popular authority and an established system of institutional and representational mechanisms and its elite members" still "provides a common conceptual starting point to capture the international features of populism" (Löfflmann, 2022, pp. 406–407).

However, despite this deeply entrenched view of populism as a local phenomenon assuming a hostile stance toward globalization, an increasing number of scholars tend to think nowadays that "it would be a mistake to simply equate populism with nationalism, isolationism, and protectionism" (Verbeek & Zaslove, 2017, p. 12). Because "good/pure people," which populists strive to represent, may or may not reside within any given country's borders, populist orientations may or may not be isolationist. Different types of populism range from exclusively isolationist policies to more open positions regarding cosmopolitanism and international institutions. To a large extent, the divergence in positions along the "isolationism–internationalism" continuum is explained by the fact that populism is a "thin" ideology: One "whose morphological structure is restricted to a set of core concepts which alone are unable to provide a reasonably broad, if not comprehensive, range of answers to the political questions that societies generate" (Stanley, 2008, p. 99). Due to their conceptual poverty, thin ideologies usually coexist with full ideologies such as liberalism or socialism. As De Cleen and colleagues put it, "a populist logic can be invoked to further very different political goals, from radical left to right" (2018, p. 649). In other words, populism can occur anywhere along the ideological spectrum; it may be left-wing, right-wing, or centrist.

Depending on the ideology they adhere to, populists may be expected to differ as to how open or protectionist their views are on policy issues. The populist right tends to be more isolationist and the populist left more cosmopolitan, while market populists, who embrace a laissez-faire ideology, tend to be more open to regionalism and economic globalization (Sawer & Laycock,

2009; Weyland, 1999). Market populists believe that implementing a truly open market liberated from state interventions would benefit the people. In the view of market populists, state bureaucrats who represent the interests of special groups deprive the people of the benefits of a true market economy. To a greater or lesser extent, market populists are open to multilateralism and do not necessarily oppose transborder migration. This type of populism partly applies to this book as it analyzes the populism of Ukrainian President Volodymyr Zelensky, who has been implementing neoliberal economic reforms since he came to power in 2019 (Baysha, 2022a).

Populist agents also differ as to how they construct their "people." As Cas Mudde and Rovira Kaltwasser (2013) note, right-wing populism tends to be exclusionary while left-wing populism is often inclusionary. The people of the former are usually defined in nativist terms and imagined residing within national or even narrower regional borders; the people of the latter are often understood in transnational terms and presented as global communities of the exploited.

The type of populism discussed in this book also appeals to a transnational community of people, only in Zelensky's case this community consists not of the oppressed but of "the civilized"—those who value democracy and liberalism, the enshrined attributes of Western modernity, and who oppose the "tyranny" and "barbarism" of Russia, as Zelensky defines the excluded "other" of his civilizational populist project (see Chapter 3). In his presentation, Ukraine appears as a "gateway to Europe" that barbarians "want to break" (Zelensky, 2022b).

Today's prevailing international challenges offer an opportunity for populists to redefine or expand their notions not only of the people but also of the elite. As Daniel Wajner (2022) argues, "both left-wing and right-wing populists may find their own transnational 'others' to alienate" (p. 425)—through nativism and ethnoreligious xenophobia, socioeconomic classification, or other criteria. For right-wing populists, the prime enemy would be globalism and/or regionalism; for left-wing populists, capitalism and/or neoliberalism; for market populists, state bureaucracy and/or leftism. However, any of these populist types may target either transnational culprits (such as global financial elites, the leaders of other states, and international institutions of government) or local villains (such as state agencies, national governments, and local politicians). In other words, while working out their positions toward domestic issues with transnational dimensions, populists may reformulate their conception of the "enemies of the people." Both empty signifiers (Laclau, 2005, see Chapter 2)—"the enemy" and "the people"—may acquire different meanings in different populist contexts.

Within the context of Ukraine discussed in this book, the civilizational populism of the Euromaidan revolution of 2014 constructed its "excluded others" domestically (see Chapter 1). These were oligarchs and their marionettes, corrupted politicians—"old elites" or "political pensioners," as Zelensky put it (Viedrov, 2022, p. 9). However, after Russia started its "special military operation" (SMO) against Ukraine in February 2022, the orientation of Zelensky's populism changed—it became explicitly transnational. "We are at the epicenter of the confrontation of two ideas. The European, democratic idea that freedom and life matter, and the cruel, tyrannical idea that what matters is a man who can subjugate other people" (Zelensky, 2022e)—this representation of the conflict by the Ukrainian president has been very typical in his discourse, with "we" referring to the transnational community of civilized people opposing Russian despotism (see Chapter 3).

According to Wajner (2022), populists may be prompted to "go abroad" by multiple strategic, psychological, and ideological incentives when a need for legitimation cannot be satisfied domestically. In this view, "going abroad" has become an intrinsic part of the electoral politics of populists who are "trapped in their inability to legitimise themselves at the national level and are therefore driven to find a legitimating escape by projecting the categories of 'people' and 'elites' transnationally" (Wajner, 2022, p. 417). By doing so, they engage in a two-level game of combining internal and external dynamics of legitimation. In other words, populists may "go out" when various legitimation traps jeopardize their political survival at home—when they need a "kind of psychological reaffirmation that their leadership is 'right'; that they alone represent the singular will of 'the people'" (Wajner, 2022, p. 424).

This two-level strategy is employed nowadays by many populist parties that strive to create transnational alliances to push forward their agendas, as in the case of populists struggling against transnational institutions of power, when right-wing and left-wing populists may even act in unison. However, as the case study discussed in this book suggests, populists may create alliances not only with their populist counterparts but also with non-populist agents (leaders and populations of other states). As my analysis of Zelensky's speeches addressing foreign audiences presented in this book shows, with the beginning of the SMO—or the "full-fledged war" between Russia and Ukraine, as the Ukrainian state narrative dubs it—his aim became the creation of a global coalition of "civilizational forces" against "tyranny" and "barbarism." Zelensky's discursive creations have constructed the people of Ukraine as an inherent part of a global civilized community that he presents himself as striving to represent. "The free must support the free. Decent people should support decent people. The conscientious must support the conscientious," he argues (Zelensky, 2022c), thus uniting Ukrainians and all people of goodwill in one transnational collective. "We are uniting the world around the truth," he claims (Zelensky, 2022d).

Such a transnational construction of "the people" is reminiscent of the then U.S. President George W. Bush's infamous dictum following the 9/11 attacks: "Either you are with us, or you are with the terrorists." However, Zelensky's effort to construct a global community of civilized people opposing barbarians appears to be a systematic strategy of utmost practical significance. In contrast to the United States in 2001, Ukraine is desperately dependent on the financial and military help of foreign governments. Because of this, international legitimation of his war effort is crucial for Zelensky, as is the affirmation of his leadership on a global scale. His construction of the Ukrainian people as bearing a "historical mission" of "pulling Europe out of the abyss" and "saving it" from Russia's barbaric onslaught (Zelensky, 2022a) has allowed Zelensky to legitimize his appeal to all "people of goodwill" to support Ukraine by any means possible, such as sanctioning Russia, supplying Ukraine with weapons and financial support, and so forth.

An important question that concerns many researchers nowadays is whether populists "going out" may be contributing to a shift toward more conflictual international relations. This concern arises logically from populism's tendency to portray the world in simplistic terms of good versus evil ("civilization" vs. "barbarism" in the case discussed in this book), making populist officials less willing to negotiate and compromise, and more inclined to embrace personalized power as an embodiment of the popular will. Empirical research confirms that populists also tend to centralize and personalize foreign policymaking (Destradi & Plagemann, 2019). Domestically, such centralization and personalization of decision-making exacerbate social polarization, strengthen authoritarian tendencies in government, and worsen the quality of the democratic condition (Levitsky & Ziblatt, 2018). One may logically assume that populists "going abroad" with an aim of creating international alliances against common enemies may increase polarization on the international stage, although some scholars believe that populists are not necessarily expected to take more aggressive foreign policy stances in an indiscriminate manner. As stated earlier, their antagonistic view of the world and policy decisions stemming from it may be mitigated by the "thick" ideologies they adhere to (Destradi & Plagemann, 2019, p. 717).

Transnational Populism and the Ukraine–Russia War of 2022

The question of a possible nexus between the civilizational/transnational populism of Zelensky and the exacerbation of the ongoing conflict—the inability to solve it by diplomatic means—is central to the discussion presented in this book, although it may seem inappropriate at first. After all, it was Russia that attacked Ukraine in February 2022, and the effort to create an international coalition to thwart Russia's aims looks perfectly reasonable and justified, despite the global polarization it may provoke. However, because this book is written in the tradition of discourse studies, an assumption it conveys is that any representation of social reality is not objective truth but a product of discursive categorizations, all of which are historically and culturally specific, and thus contingent (Laclau & Mouffe, 1985).

The condition of possibility for a full-fledged discourse to take shape, gain strength, and be accepted as a normal judgment is the exclusion of alternative meanings and the "others" who express them. This is important to recognize because the construction of discourses through the exclusion of otherness delimits what is meaningful to discuss, the ways it can be discussed, and the political actions stemming from these discussions. The myth of "civilization and democracy fighting against tyranny and barbarism," as propagated by Zelensky, is only one possible way to characterize the ongoing war; the possibility of alternative articulations also exists. In the context of contemporary war-torn Ukraine, however, these articulations are excluded from the field of political representation: Oppositional parties are banned, oppositional media outlets are shut down, and some oppositional journalists and bloggers are arrested while others have been forced to flee Ukraine (Baysha, 2022b; Cohen, 2022; Myrolyb, 2022; Yasinsky, 2022; more on this in Chapters 4–6).

To be sure, Zelensky's war on journalism started long before the current war. On February 2, 2021, the Ukrainian president signed sanctions by the National Security and Defense Council (NSDC) against two parliamentary deputies from "Opposition Platform—For Life" (OPZZh), the main political rival of his own party. As a result of this unconstitutional move, three television channels controlled by the opposition—NewsOne, 112 Ukraine, and ZIK—were shut down. This happened after Zelensky's approval rating, sinking throughout the course of his unpopular neoliberal reforms, fell below 30 percent, for which he blamed oppositional media (2022b). In the official discourse, however, the closure of the oppositional channels was linked to investigation of their owners' alleged involvement in "financing terrorism"—that is, their economic relations with the Donetsk People's Republic (DPR) and Luhansk People's Republic (LPR), separatist quasi-states that announced their independence from Ukraine in 2014 in the aftermath of the Euromaidan revolution (see Chapter 1).

Given that accusations of terrorism have been used as a perennial tactic by authoritarian leaders seeking to quash political dissent and suppress freedom of expression (Pokalova, 2010), international press freedom watchdogs did not welcome Zelensky's move (IFJ, 2021; RSF, 2021). Matilda Bogner, the head of the UN Human Rights Monitoring Mission in Ukraine, argued that "the state must respect, protect and provide the right for freedom of expression" (Radiosvoboda, 2021a). "Ukraine's efforts to protect its territorial integrity and national security, as well as to defend itself from information manipulation are legitimate, but . . . this should not come at the expense of freedom of media," the spokesperson of EU foreign policy chief Josep Borrell maintained (RFE/RL, 2021).

Zelensky, however, had no intention of backing down. In August 2021, Strana.ua—another popular oppositional media outlet—was accused of spreading "anti-Ukrainian propaganda" and sanctioned by the NSDC (Ukrainska Pravda, 2021). In December 2021, new sanctions were signed against the companies that owned the newly established channels First Independent Channel and UKRLIVE (Reaney, 2021). The oppositional television channel

Nash, whose popularity had grown steadily since the closure of 112 Ukraine, ZIK, and NewsOne (Radiosvoboda, 2021b), was shut down by an NSDC decision on February 11, 2022.

The onset of Russia's attack against Ukraine on February 24, 2022, prompted another round of efforts to crush dissent, expanding on what had come earlier. On March 20, 2022, Zelensky signed a decision by the NSDC to ban 11 oppositional political parties. In parallel, he also implemented the NSDC's decision to launch a telethon called "United News #UARAZOM," which all national TV channels were expected to broadcast (Harding, 2022). All oppositional meanings have since come to be seen as "Russian disinformation," with the arrests of oppositional journalists and bloggers justified by the necessity of defending the sovereignty of Ukraine and punishing "traitors" (see Chapters 4–6). Many oppositionists were lucky enough to have made it out of Ukraine, and now work in exile.

Clearly, antagonistic discourses have taken hold on both sides of the conflict—a typical situation in wartime. Russian authorities have also been attempting to shut down oppositional discourses and stabilize meanings favorable to their political course. On the very first day of the SMO, Roskomnadzor, the Federal Service for Supervision of Communications, Information Technology and Mass Media, published an announcement instructing Russian media to disseminate only "reliable and up-to-date information" (Roskomnadzor, 2022). The dissemination of "fake information" would lead to media blocking, it warned. On March 4, 2022, the State Duma adopted several amendments to the Criminal Code and to the Code of Administrative Offences of the Russian Federation (OIPLI, 2022). Now, those accused of spreading "false" information regarding the SMO may be punished with fines or prison terms.

Meanwhile, the Russian Ministry of Education prepared a manual explaining what the state accepts as "the truth": The SMO was launched to prevent the fundamental threat that the West created for Russian consistency; to prevent NATO from expanding to Russia's borders; to denazify and demilitarize Ukraine; and to protect Russian people living in Ukraine (Kommersant, 2022a). These and other reasons for the war presented in the manual were based on Vladimir Putin's speech on February 24 (Kremlin, 2022a). To stabilize the meanings highlighted by Putin, Roskomnadzor has blocked within Russian territory numerous domestic and foreign media outlets, including the BBC, Deutsche Welle, *Meduza*, Echo of Moscow, and others. On March 16, 2022, Putin commented on Russia's policy of silencing Russian oppositional voices by calling them "scum" and "traitors" that Russia must get rid of to "purify" itself: "Any people, and especially the Russian people, will always be able to distinguish true patriots from scum and traitors. . . . I am convinced that such a natural and necessary self-purification of society will only strengthen our country" (Kremlin, 2022b, 20:05–20:27).

Arrests and imprisonment came to be used in dealing with such "traitors." Among the most well-known journalists against whom criminal cases have been opened are Valery Badmaev, editor-in-chief of *Modern Kalmykia*; Yevgeny Domozhirov, editor-in-chief of SOTAvision; Dmitry Golubovsky, editor-in-chief of Radio Arzamas; and Vladimir Kara-Murza Jr., a journalist and oppositional activist. In December 2022, the oppositionist Ilya Yashin, accused of spreading fakes about the Russian army, was sentenced to eight years and six months in a general regime colony (BBC, 2022). To avoid Yashin's fate, oppositional media companies preferred to leave Russia. Many foreign media—such as ABC, Bloomberg, the CBC, CBS, CNN, Condé Nast, and others—stopped their work in Russia so as not to jeopardize the well-being of their employees (Kommersant, 2022b).

All these recent developments within the Russian media sphere are similar to what has been going on in Ukraine. However, there is a significant difference between the two cases. On a global level, the Russian official war-related narrative—that the war is an attempt to defend the Russian-speaking population of Ukraine and prevent NATO from establishing itself on Russia's borders—has remained rather marginal. For the most part, it has been given serious consideration only by alternative media and isolated critical thinkers (e.g., Boyd-Barrett, 2022; Mearsheimer, 2022). In contrast, the Ukrainian state narrative—about Russia attacking Ukraine to trample democracy and civilization—has been hegemonized by mainstream Western politicians and media with a global reach (Bishara, 2022; Counter Signal, 2022). It is exactly this narrative that Zelensky has been propagating in his interviews with ABC, the BBC, CBS, CNN, the *Economist*, Netflix, PBS, *Time*, the *Washington Post*, and others. These media platforms have been providing Zelensky with an unlimited opportunity to deliver his message to global publics with an aim of creating an anti-Russian coalition of the "civilized world." Zelensky's "propaganda value spilled well beyond Ukraine, as he made speech after speech to the 'world community' (countries not aligned with Russia and China), which fell in line," as John Hartley put it (2023, pp. 13–14)

According to the presidential YouTube channel, from February 24 to October 11, 2022 (the day he addressed the G-7 after Russia's massive missile attack against Ukrainian infrastructure, which marked the beginning of a new phase of the conflict), Zelensky delivered 128 speeches to foreign audiences and gave 26 interviews (including press conferences) to foreign media. He has been using these opportunities to discursively create his transnational "people" (see Chapter 3). This is a unique case of transnational populism, as no other state leader has ever been engaged in so many international media performances on a daily basis. Among other things, this unusual case is worth investigating because it involves worldwide normalization of an extremely simplified definition of an issue of global significance—a regional war with a nuclear power that could lead to disastrous outcomes for the whole world.

Within the mentioned time period, I analyzed all the speeches Zelensky delivered to international audiences (N=128) and all his interviews given to foreign media (N=26); both the speeches and the interviews were accessed on the presidential website. I also analyzed all meetings between Zelensky and Ukrainian journalists, held within the same period of time (N=4), to identify differences in Zelensky's discursive construction of the situation for domestic and foreign audiences. For the purposes of my investigation, a discourse analysis informed by the discourse theory of Ernesto Laclau and Chantal Mouffe (1985) has been employed. The results of this analysis have been interpreted by drawing on the theory of populism as developed by Laclau (2005) and the conception of antagonistic discourse by Nico Carpentier (2017).

To deconstruct the "common sense" of the "democracy and civilization versus tyranny and barbarism" discourse propagated by Zelensky, I have incorporated into my analysis alternative articulations of the Ukrainian crisis by oppositional voices that have been removed from the field of political representation within Ukraine. The activation of oppositional outlooks makes it possible to see the contingency of Zelensky's populist discourse, which leaves aside many important factors that need to be accounted for to understand the conflict. Among those "excluded others" whose discursive constructions are analyzed in the book are Oles Buzina, a publicist killed by Ukrainian radicals; Ruslan Kotsaba and Dmitry Vasilets, journalists who served prison terms for "treason"; Dmitry Dzhangirov, Yuri Tkachev, and Andrei Wojciechowski, journalists arrested in the spring of 2022 for "anti-Ukrainian activities"; and Tatyana Montyan, Anatoliy Sharij, and Taras Nezalezhko, popular bloggers now working in exile. Among many other journalists and bloggers who have been repressed in Ukraine after the Euromaidan (see Chapter 1) and the beginning of the SMO, I have selected these figures because I know them personally (Dzhangirov, Montyan, Tkachev, and Wojciechowski) and/or have been following their publications for years (Kotsaba, Vasilets, Nezalezhko, and Sharij).[1]

Unlike my analysis of all of Zelensky's speeches and interviews during a given time span, I chose only the most representative examples of writing or commentary by oppositionists so as to illuminate some of the most important points ignored by Zelensky in his articulations of the crisis. In addition, in the case of Dzhangirov, Sharij, and Tkachev—because they were "canceled" (arrested or banned) after the beginning of the ongoing war—I have also conducted a systematic analysis of their posts from February 24 to the days of their respective arrests (Dzhangirov and Tkachev) or bans (Sharij). Within this period, all their posts were monitored daily.

The book is divided into two parts. The first part presents the background of the crisis (Chapter 1), the theoretical-methodological foundations of my research (Chapter 2), and the analysis of Zelensky's war-related discourse (Chapter 3). The second part of the book considers oppositional articulations and discusses the three most important nodal points that are necessary to take into account for understanding the Ukrainian crisis: external control over Ukraine (Chapter 4), Ukraine's deep societal split and the prosecution of dissent (Chapter 5), and Ukraine's non-implementation of the Minsk agreements (Chapter 6).

The main argument presented in the book is twofold. First, the simplistic, one-dimensional representations of social reality leave no space for understanding complex conflicts and have little, if any, potential to bring about peace. Second, to destabilize the one-dimensionality of populist discourses and enrich our vision regarding complex societal developments, we need to incorporate into analysis the alternative articulations that are commonly excluded from the field of political representation by authoritarian populism.

Note

1 I know many oppositional journalists and bloggers personally because I am originally from Ukraine (I am an ethnic Ukrainian, and most of my relatives still reside in Ukraine) and worked as a journalist there from 1991—the first year of Ukraine's independence—to 2008, when I started my doctoral studies at the University of Colorado at Boulder. I came to live in Russia in the fall of 2013, the year of the Euromaidan, in the aftermath of which many Russian-speaking journalists holding anti-Maidan views had to flee Ukraine to avoid the destiny of Oles Buzina and other victims of the revolution (see Chapters 4 and 5).

Reference List

Baysha, O. (2022a). *Democracy, populism, and neoliberalism in Ukraine: On the fringes of the virtual and the real.* Routledge.

Baysha, O. (2022b). On the impossibility of discursive-material closures: A case of banned TV channels in Ukraine. *Social Sciences & Humanities Open*, 6(1), 1–7. doi:10.1016/j.ssaho.2022.100329

BBC. (2022). *Ilya Yashin was sentenced to 8.5 years in the case of "military fakes"* (In Russian). www.bbc.com/russian/news-63864402

Biegon, R. (2019). A populist grand strategy? Trump and the framing of American decline. *International Relations*, 33(4), 517–539. doi:10.1177/0047117819852399

Bishara, M. (2022, August 4). Western media and the war on truth in Ukraine. *AlJazeera*. www.aljazeera.com/opinions/2022/8/4/western-media-and-the-war-on-truth-in

Boyd-Barrett, O. (2022, February 18). NATO, Russia and Ukraine: False pretexts for war. *Canadian Dimension*. https://canadiandimension.com/articles/view/nato-russia-and-ukraine-false-pretexts-for-war

Carpentier, N. (2017). *The discursive-material knot: Cyprus in conflict and community media participation.* Peter Lang.

Chryssogelos, A. (2020). State transformation and populism: From the internationalized to the neo-Sovereign state? *Politics*, 40(1), 22–37. doi:10.1177/0263395718803830

Cohen, D. (2022, April 14). Testimony reveals Zelensky's secret police plot. *MPN News*. www.mintpressnews.com/volodymyr-zelensky-secret-police-hunted-down-opposition-anatoly-shariy/280200/

Counter Signal. (2022, October 18). *Keean Bexte offered thousands to push pro-Ukraine propaganda.* https://thecountersignal.com/keean-bexte-offered-thousands-to-push-pro-ukraine-propaganda/

De Cleen, B., Glynos, J., & Mondon, A. (2018). Critical research on populism: Nine rules of engagement. *Organization, 25*(5), 649–661. doi:10.1177/1350508418768053

De Cleen, B., Moffitt, B., Panayotu, P., et al. (2020). The potentials and difficulties of transnational populism: The case of the democracy in Europe movement 2025 (DiEM25). *Political Studies, 68*(1), 146–166. doi:10.1177/0032321719847576

De la Torre, C. (2018). *Routledge handbook of global populism*. Routledge.

Destradi, S., & Plagemann, J. (2019). Populism and international relations:(Un)predictability, personalisation, and the reinforcement of existing trends in world politics. *Review of International Studies, 45*(5), 711–730. doi:10.1017/S026021051 9000184

Fraser, N. (2019). *The old is dying and the new cannot be born: From progressive neoliberalism to Trump and beyond*. Verso.

Grzymala-Busse, A. (2019). Conclusion: The global forces of populism. *Polity, 51*(4), 718–723. doi:10.1086/705322

Hadiz, V. R., & Chryssogelos, A. (2017). Populism in world politics: A comparative cross- regional perspective. *International Political Science Review, 38*(4), 399–411. doi:10.1177/0192512117693908

Harding, L. (2022, March 20). Ukraine suspends 11 political parties with links to Russia. *Guardian*. www.theguardian.com/world/2022/mar/20/ukraine-suspends-11-political-parties-with-links-to-russia

Hartley, J. (2023). Strategic stories: Weaponized or worldmaking? *Global Media and China*. Online before print. doi:10.1177/20594364231153200

Harvey, D. (2018). Universal alienation. *TripleC, 16*(2), 424–439. doi:10.31269/triplec. v16i2.1026

IFJ. (2021, February 3). Ukraine: President bans three television channels. *International Federation of Journalists*. www.ifj.org/media-centre/news/detail/category/press-releases/article/ukraine-president-bans-three-television-channels.html

Jahn, B. (2018). Liberal internationalism: Historical trajectory and current prospects. *International Affairs, 94*(1), 43–61. doi:10.1093/ia/iix231

Judis, J. (2016). *The populist explosion: How the great recession transformed American and European politics*. Columbia Global Reports.

Kommersant. (2022a). *Answers sent to teachers*. www.kommersant.ru/doc/5239256

Kommersant. (2022b). *Which foreign business interrupted work in Russia*. www.kommersant.ru/doc/5240137

Kremlin. (2022a). *Addresses of the President of the Russian federation* (In Russian). www.youtube.com/watch?v=sIPIMD9sPhA

Kremlin. (2022b). *Opening remarks at the meeting on measures of socio-economic support for the regions* (In Russian). www.youtube.com/watch?v=HLEezN2qLh0

Laclau, E. (2005). *On populist reason*. Verso.

Laclau, E., & Mouffe, C. (1985). *Hegemony and socialist strategy: Towards a radical democratic politics*. Verso.

Levitsky, S., & Ziblatt, D. (2018). *How democracies die*. Broadway Books.

Löfflmann, G. (2022). Introduction to special issue: The study of populism in international relations. *The British Journal of Politics and International Relations, 24*(3), 403–415. doi:10.1177/13691481221103116

Mearsheimer, J. (2022, June 16). The causes and consequences of the Ukraine war. *YouTube*. www.youtube.com/watch?v=qciVozNtCDM&t=750s

Moffitt, B. (2017). Transnational populism? Representative claims, media and the difficulty of constructing a transnational 'people'. *Javnost, 24*(4), 409–425. doi:10.108 0/13183222.2017.1330086

Mudde, C., & Kaltwasser, C. R. (2013). Exclusionary vs. inclusionary populism: Comparing con temporary Europe and Latin America. *Government and Opposition, 48*(2), 147–174. doi:10.1017/gov.2012.11

Mudde, C., & Kaltwasser, C. R. (2017). *Populism: A very short introduction*. Oxford University Press.

Müller, J. W. (2017). *What is populism?* Penguin.

Myrolyb, S. (2022, March 19). Kyiv's unobserved war against dissident public intellectuals. *New Cold War*. https://newcoldwar.org/kyivs-unobserved-war-against-dissident-public-intellectuals/

OIPLI. (2022). *The federal law dated 04/03/2022* (in Russian). Official Internet Portal of Legal Information. http://publication.pravo.gov.ru/Document/View/00012022030 40007?index=0&rangeSize =1

Pokalova, E. (2010). Framing separatism as terrorism: Lessons from Kosovo. *Studies in Conflict and Terrorism, 33*(5), 429–447. doi:10.1080/10576101003691564

Radiosvoboda. (2021a, March 11). *UN on the ban of Medvedchuk's channels*. www.radiosvoboda.org/a/news-kanaly-medvedchuka/31145169.html

Radiosvoboda. (2021b, May 2). *Alternatively pro-Russian: How 'Nash' TV channel works*. www.radiosvoboda.org/a/telekanal-nash-i-rosijski-naratyvy/31233497.html

Reaney, L. (2021, December 29). Media whack-a-mole: Zelensky smacks Medvedchuk's new channels. *Kyiv Post*. www.kyivpost.com/ukraine-politics/media-whack-a-mole-zelensky-smacks-medvedchuks-new-channels.html

RFE/RL. (2021, February 3). *EU questions Ukrainian president's sanctions on TV stations*. www.rferl.org/a/eu-questions-ukrainian-sanctions-tv-stations-medvedchuk-zelenskiy/31084591.html

Roskomnadzor. (2022). *To the attention of the media and other information resources* (in Russian). https://rkn.gov.ru/news/rsoc/news74084.htm

RSF. (2021, February 26). Ukraine escalates 'information war' by banning three pro-Kremlin media. *Reporters Without Borders*. https://rsf.org/en/news/ukraine-escalates-information-war-banning-threepro-kremlin-media

Sawer, M., & Laycock, D. (2009). Down with elites and up with inequality: Market populism in Australia and Canada. *Commonwealth and Comparative Politics, 47*(2), 133–150. doi:10.1080/14662040902842836

Stanley, B. (2008). The thin ideology of populism. *Journal of Political Ideologies, 13*(1), 95–110.

Ukrainska Pravda. (2021, August 20). *National security and defense council has imposed sanctions against Shariy and Guzhva*. www.pravda.com.ua/news/2021/08/20/7304526

Verbeek, B., & Zaslove, A. (2017). Populism and foreign policy. In *The Oxford handbook of populism* (pp. 384–405). doi:10.1093/oxfordhb/9780198803560.013.15

Viedrov, O. (2022). Back-to-normality outsiders: Zelensky's technocratic populism, 2019–2021. *East European Politics*, online before print, 1–24. doi:10.1080/21599 165.2022.2146092

Voeten, E. (2020). Populism and backlashes against international courts. *Perspectives on Politics, 18*(2), 407–422. https://doi.org/10.1017/S1537592719000975

Wajner, D. (2022). The populist way out: Why contemporary populist leaders seek transnational legitimation. *The British Journal of Politics and International Relations, 24*(3), 416–436. doi:10.1177/13691481211069345

Weyland, K. (1999). Neoliberal populism in Latin America and Eastern Europe. *Comparative Politics*, *31*(4), 379–401. doi:10.2307/422236

Yasinsky, O. (2022, March 21). Witchhunt in Ukraine against journalists. *Pressenza*. www.pressenza.com/2022/03/witchhunt-in-ukraine-against-journalists-activists-and-left-wing-politicians/?fbclid=IwAR2Q6V5qxNBFmwd1OQm-NLj1UxJyxxw NSMyKn9pqE7xkDDHhQ9DRJbubeN8&mibextid=ATveJy

Zelensky, V. (2022a, March 11). Volodymyr Zelensky's address to Polish Sejm (in Ukrainian). *YouTube*. www.youtube.com/watch?v=qyfOUVmX3Kw

Zelensky, V. (2022b, March 22). Volodymyr Zelensky addressed the people and politicians of Italy (in Ukrainian). *YouTube*. www.youtube.com/watch?v=Anmx0rvpFZA

Zelensky, V. (2022c, April 21). To the Portuguese. The address of Ukraine's President Volodymyr Zelensky (in Ukrainian). *YouTube*. www.youtube.com/watch?v=fjfe7 XnglkE

Zelensky, V. (2022d, May 6). President Zelensky participated in a conference of UK analytical centers at Chatham House (in Ukrainian). *YouTube*. www.youtube.com/watch?v=XrQzIm1O0UU

Zelensky, V. (2022e, May 10). To Slovaks. President Zelensky' address (in Ukrainian). *YouTube*. www.youtube.com/watch?v=23hePSuKJF4

Žižek, S. (2018). The prospects of radical change today. *TripleC*, *16*(2), 476–489. doi:10.31269/triplec.v16i2.1023

Part I

Populist Discourse of Civilization

1 From the Euromaidan to the Russia–Ukraine War
2013–2022

The Euromaidan and Its Excluded "Others"

Although this book is about the Russia–Ukraine war of 2022, I will start with a brief overview of the Euromaidan revolution and its social consequences. Understanding what happened in Ukraine in 2013–2014 and how the complexity of the Ukrainian crisis has been simplified and distorted in political and media representations is crucial for understanding the ongoing military conflict (Matveeva, 2022; Petro, 2022).

The Euromaidan (also "the Maidan") started on November 21, 2013, after the Ukrainian journalist Mustafa Nayem put out a call on Facebook for people to gather in Maidan Square in Kyiv. The idea was to press President Victor Yanukovych to sign an Association Agreement with the European Union.[1] The signing of the document was expected to happen at the third summit of the Eastern Partnership in Vilnius, on November 28–29, 2013. The efforts of those gathered on the Maidan—initially, a rather small group of young people—were in vain. Yanukovych refused to sign the agreement, arguing that he could not afford to sacrifice trade with Russia, which opposed the deal. On November 30, police dispersed the Maidan protesters; some of them were beaten.

In the eyes of millions of Ukrainians, Yanukovych personified a corrupt and inefficient regime; after the violent dispersal of the protesters, he seemed to them a brutal dictator. Kyiv exploded with protest. On December 1, tens of thousands gathered in the center of the Ukrainian capital to say "no" to the cruelty of the Yanukovych regime. Demonstrators carried a huge banner of the European Union and chanted "Ukraine is Europe"; they were greeted from the podium not only by the leaders of the Ukrainian opposition but also by European politicians (Baysha, 2018).

December 1 was the day the Kyiv City State Administration and other administrative buildings were occupied by the members of the nationalist party "Svoboda"[2] and other radicals. The first violent clashes between these groups and police took place during the storming of the governmental district, when police officers were attacked by radicals with smoke bombs, stones,

DOI: 10.4324/9781003379164-3

and chains.[3] After that day, the clashes between protesters and police intensified, with pictures and videos of burning police—torched with Molotov cocktails—quickly becoming iconic.

The fighting reached a climax on February 18–20, when dozens of people were killed on both sides. Following these tragic events, an agreement on the settlement of the political crisis in the presence of high-ranking European officials was signed. According to this agreement, Yanukovych was supposed to stay in power until early presidential elections. However, Maidan radicals ran roughshod over the results of the negotiations, and Yanukovych was ousted from power. On February 22, with Yanukovych having managed to flee Ukraine for Russia, Olexander Turchynov became the acting president of Ukraine. The overturning of the regime in power was complete.

Many argue that Maidan protesters saw the agreement with the European Union as a means to escape from the corrupted system of the Yanukovych government and achieve a more democratic condition (Åslund, 2015; Kuzio, 2017; Wilson, 2014). With respect to some percentage of Maidan participants, this is obviously true. However, there is an important aspect of the revolution that is usually overlooked: the deeply mythological structure of its hegemonic discourse, which may explain—at least to some extent—the animosity between the two Ukraines (pro-Maidan and anti-Maidan) that developed during the Maidan confrontation (Baysha, 2015). "Ukraine is occupied by the Golden Horde"; "If in Bible times a mountain could move from one place to another, why cannot this happen now?"; "The Christmas Story goes on. The tyrant was killing children but could not overcome the creation of Good and its victory over the Devil"; "The holy defender of Kyiv, God's messenger with the sword of fire, is with us!"—in the representations of Maidan activists, such mythological constructions were omnipresent (Baysha, 2018, pp. 118–129).

Among some of the revolutionaries, the belief in their cause as a fight between good and evil was so strong that they imagined the protesters as "the army of light" that "stormed the sky" and created a "Bible miracle" by "separating the Light from the Darkness" (Bistritsky, 2013). Rather than the democratic aspirations held by some portion of the Maidan participants, it is this revolutionary exaltation that can explain, at least partially, the activists' anger not only toward anti-Maidan Ukrainians, which they treated in chauvinist terms (see below), but also against Russia.

For those Euromaidan activists who equated their cause with the struggle of the forces of light against the forces of evil, any union with Russia, for the sake of which Yanukovych sacrificed the agreement with the EU, was the end of Ukraine's road to the European future imagined as a mythical Kingdom of Ends (Baysha, 2018). It is here that the positions of Maidan liberals and radical nationalists, who ensured the victory of the revolution by seizing administrative buildings and taking up arms (Katchanovski, 2016), converged: The latter supported the Maidan not because of democratization, liberalization, or romanticism but due to its clear anti-Russia stance (Sakwa, 2015). The fact that half of Ukraine did not support the revolution was of little interest to these radicals. As for liberals, many of them simply could not believe there were "normal people" who did not support the uprising: This was beyond the limits of the thinkable as set by their progressive imaginary presenting the revolution as a fight between the forces of good and evil (Baysha, 2016).

To understand what happened in Ukraine in the aftermath of the revolution, one needs to acknowledge that in February 2014, when people were dying in the streets of Kyiv in the name of European integration, the support for this integration across the country was no higher than 41 percent (KIIS, 2015). Regional differences were distinct (Kull, 2015). The farther east one looked, the stronger and more unified a rejection of the Euromaidan with its European agenda one would find (KIIS, 2014). More than 75 percent of those living in the Donetsk and Luhansk oblasts (two eastern regions of Ukraine predominantly populated by Russian speakers) rejected the agreement with the EU; many of them believed that the Euromaidan revolution was an "armed coup d'état organized by the opposition with the help of the West" and did not approve of Euromaidan revolutionaries using weapons against police forces (KIIS, 2014). Only 20 percent of the people living in Crimea supported the Euromaidan, while 71 percent were against it (Kush, 2014).

Remarkably, although roughly half the country was against the overturning of the government then in power, Euromaidan activists put themselves forward as representing the whole of Ukraine. Maidan leaders equated their protesters with the general population of the country, ignoring millions of Ukrainians who did not share their views (Baysha, 2020c). "Honorable people of Ukraine!" and "Dear Ukrainian community!"—this is how the revolution's most prominent figures addressed protesters from the main podium at the Maidan. None of them problematized this constructed equivalence between "the people of Ukraine" and "the people of the Maidan"; in all their representations, the former and the latter were seen as wholly the same. "Today, all the country, from the West to the East, unanimously demands the resignation of the government," claimed Yuri Lutsenko (2013, 3:55–64:01), who went on to become a post-Maidan Prosecutor General of Ukraine. What these and endless similar constructions unambiguously suggested was that "the other Ukraine"—the one that did not support the revolution—simply did not exist.

But how was it logically possible to ignore an anti-Maidan population so large it amounted to half the country? The condition through which this occurred was the ascribing of a lower moral/intellectual status to Ukrainian citizens who did not support the revolution; they were seen as "sovki" ("sovok" in singular)[4] and "vatniki" ("vatnik" in singular)[5] who did not deserve to be part of the community of "Ukrainian people," a term equated with Ukrainian Maidan supporters. As Irina Farion (2014, 1:02–11:22), one of the leading figures of "Svoboda," put it, "We are persistent in our aim to build a free, unitary, self-sufficient, and invincible Ukraine. Lackeys, plebeians, slaves . . . will never understand this." According to this logic, accepted by most Euromaidan activists as common sense, only "unworthy" people whose opinions should be ignored could refrain from supporting the uprising.

From the very beginning of the Euromaidan, its supporters cast anti-Maidan "others" as the constitutive outside not only of the Maidan movement but also of Ukraine. As the activist Dmytro Sinchenko (2014) put it, "Since the moment of Ukraine's independence, there has been a fierce information and worldview war—the war between Ukraine and sovok." According to Sinchenko (2014),

> This war is internal, and it has divided the territory of Ukraine in two: The front line of the struggle against sovok goes today along the border of Odessa, Mykolaiv, Kherson, Zaporizhia, Dnipropetrovsk, Kharkiv, and Luhansk regions.

Anatoliy Hrytsenko (2013), Ukraine's defense minister from 2005 to 2007, agreed:

> I am not talking about the split along the East-West line or between adherents and opponents of Euro-integration. I am talking about a more bitter and more essential phenomenon that is typical for all regions—the distinction between the people and the population; between citizens and slaves.

In these and endless other similar cases, the difference between Kyiv and the cities of Eastern Ukraine, which later became the sites of bloody battles, was imagined not in terms of a political disagreement but as a simple division between fearless fighters for the civilized future and fearful pro-Russian slaves pulling Ukraine back into the Middle Ages or "sovok." In other words, this was a fight between civilization and barbarism, or the future and the past. Any rejection of the Euromaidan caused indignation and disgust. "I am ashamed and disgusted to live in one country not simply with a few bastards but with millions of slaves"—this is how Volodymyr Dubrovsky (2013), another Euromaidan activist, saw his compatriots who opposed the Maidan. In hegemonic pro-Maidan discourse, such a representation of anti-Maidan others was normalized.

In response, anti-Maidan "others" labeled their opponents "kastry-ulegoloviye" (panheads),[6] "maidauni,"[7] and "skakuni" (jumpers)[8]—derogatory terms to denote stupidity, infantilism, and the brainwashed condition of those who supported the revolution (Baysha, 2020a, 2020b). The imagined "brainless" condition of "panheads," "maidauni," and "jumpers," as well as the underdeveloped condition of "sovki" and "vatniki," did not presuppose much possibility for meaningful communication. Instead, this mutual antagonism led to a further ramping up of hostility, which exploded into violent confrontations during the Maidan—when torturing, lynching, and humiliating political opponents became widespread (Baysha, 2018, pp. 154–159)—and especially after the victory of the revolution.

The Donbas uprising and Odessa tragedy (to be discussed in Chapter 5) occurred amid this spiral of mutual hatred among pro-Maidan and anti-Maidan Ukrainians, with each event only intensifying the conflict further. "With the passage of time," one of the UN's numerous reports on the situation suggested, "divisions in Ukrainian society resulting from the conflict will continue to deepen and take root" (UN OHCHR, 2017, p. 40). This is exactly what has happened.

Donbas Uprising: From Anti-Maidan to Separatism and Terrorism

Starting in late February of 2014, demonstrations protesting the coup d'état took place in Ukraine's eastern and some southern regions. From the very beginning of these manifestations, all "progressive" (i.e., pro-Maidan) media in Ukraine presented the anti-Maidan movement predominantly as "pro-Russian" and "separatist" (Baysha, 2017). Such a representation of the protesters seems plausible at first glance, given that those holding Russian national banners and chanting "Russia!" were the most vocal and visible participants in anti-Maidan meetings, and therefore attracted the lion's share of media attention. The truth behind this representation, however, is that the call to separate the southeastern regions of the country from Ukraine was not the sole demand that the participants in anti-Maidan demonstrations put forward; it was not even the main one.

Most people in the Southeast articulated their anti-Maidan struggles not as efforts to separate from Ukraine but as a rejection of the policy of cutting ties with Russia in favor of the EU and NATO. As mentioned earlier, only 41 percent of Ukrainians supported EU integration during the Maidan; the number supporting a bid to join NATO was even lower. In 2013, only 18 percent of Ukrainians wanted the country to become a member of the Western alliance (Slovoidilo, 2021). Anti-Maidan protesters advocated an economic union with Russia and wanted to conduct a referendum on federalization to enhance regional self-governance. They wanted to preserve Russian as an official language in the eastern regions of Ukraine, and they also protested the rise of nationalism, whose radical adherents were the most active Maidan fighters (KIIS, 2014).

Despite the diversity of stated motives, however, in media coverage of the anti-Maidan protests, the sign "separatism" assumed a hegemonic position representing all the varied demands linked together in a single "anti-Maidan" chain of equivalence (Laclau, 2005, see Chapter 2); moreover, it displaced the signifier "federalization." Typical representations of the anti-Maidan popular demands in pro-Maidan media went as follows (emphasis added): "In Kharkiv, *separatists* demand a referendum on the *federalization* of Ukraine" (Ukrainska Pravda, 2014a); "In Luhansk, a *separatist* meeting for *federalization* is held" (Gordon, 2014a); "In Nikolaev, *separatists* stormed the building of the Regional State Administration demanding a referendum on *federalization*"

(Leviy Bereg, 2014). Even when the media acknowledged that the "separatists" wanted federalization—not separation from Ukraine—they habitually lumped all protesting groups together under the label of "separatists."

Because "federalization" was equated with "separatism" in hegemonic Maidan discourse, the former term was juxtaposed not only to the notion of the "unitary state" but also to the "unity of Ukraine." In other words, the unity of Ukraine came to be understood only in unitary nationalistic terms: "On March 30, two meetings were held in Kharkiv: one for *federalization*, another for the *unity of Ukraine*" (Gordon, 2014b, emphasis added). All other ideas apart from unitary state organization were thus depicted as undermining the security of the Ukrainian state. Shifting the focus from "anti-Maidan" to "separatism," pro-Maidan media not only simplified and distorted the protests but also delegitimized them. On April 7, 2014, Ukraine's Prime Minister Arseniy Yatsenyuk added federalization, equated to separatism, to the list of crimes against the state: "Any calls for federalization are attempts to destroy the Ukrainian state system according to the scenario written in Russia" (Ukrainska Pravda, 2014b).

In early March of 2014, anti-Maidan militants, following the example of their pro-Maidan counterparts in Kyiv, stormed and occupied state administrative buildings in the cities of southeastern Ukraine. But unlike those in Kyiv who had been defined as "activists," the Donbas occupiers engaging in similar actions were considered "terrorists." This double standard, first by Euromaidan activists and later by the post-Maidan government, was taken as a stark injustice by many people holding anti-Maidan views and could not but fuel their resentment (Baysha, 2017). After Russia took control of Crimea as a response to the overturning of power in Kyiv, the tendency to see anti-government manifestations in southeastern regions not as democratic protests but as activities undermining national sovereignty came to be formalized in Ukraine's official discourse. As many Russian citizens participated in what they called the "Russian Spring"—a revival of the "Russian world" in the form of a "New Russia" [Новороссия]—this trend of overlooking or denying the legitimacy of the demands of Donbas people only strengthened.

There is no doubt that the Donbas insurgency was backed by Russia. The fact that Moscow sent weapons, military experts, and "volunteers" such as Strelkov (Girkin)[9] to Donbas is commonly referred to as the "Russian invasion." However, what is often lost in representing the Ukrainian crisis exclusively through this frame is that 45.3 percent of the people living in Donetsk and 55.1 percent in Luhansk justified the armed resistance against the new Kyiv government on the grounds that "during the revolution, the protesters in Kyiv and western regions did the same" and "there was no other means to attract the center's attention to the problems of the regions" (KIIS, 2014). As Nicolai Petro (2023) put it,

The most popular view then, as now, is that the country's post-Maidan crisis is entirely the result of Russian aggression. What makes this explanation less than complete, however, is that Ukraine's historical and cultural divisions are well established and have been a prominent theme in scholarly writing about the country. It is hard to imagine how they could suddenly be divorced from current events.

(p. xii)

What is often left without attention is that the roots of the Donbas insurgency were local, despite its co-opting by Russia for its own geopolitical interests. It is important to recognize that during the first stage of the conflict, in January–March 2014, the rebels "were primarily locals" (Kuzio, 2017, p. 252).

Ignoring the complex interplay of both internal and external factors at the root of the unrest in Eastern Ukraine, on April 13, 2014, then acting President Olexander Turchynov announced the beginning of the "anti-terrorist operation" (ATO), calling the occupiers of administrative buildings in Donbas "terrorists" under Russian command (Turchynov, 2014, 0:26–30:37). By the commencement of the ATO, those in power after the Euromaidan had administratively defined the anti-Maidan uprising as terrorism. This totalitarian discursive closure led to dramatic political consequences, including the effort to crush the Donbas rebellion with heavy involvement from the Ukrainian Army and radical nationalists in volunteer battalions.

In addition to causing thousands of casualties—up to 14,000 people have been killed from April 2014 to February 2022 (Crisis Group, 2022)—the ATO also radicalized the societal confrontation and reinforced nondemocratic methods of governance in both the rebel strongholds and Kyiv-controlled territories of Ukraine, strengthening radicalism on both sides (UN OHCHR, 2017). Ukraine also began blockading Crimea and Donbas economically and by other means, denying their populations access to vitally important resources such as energy and water (Matveeva, 2022, pp. 423–435). The supply of water to the North Crimean Canal, for example, which provided up to 85 percent of Crimea's water needs, was cut off by Ukraine in 2014, after Russia established control over the peninsula.

Even with the domestic tensions that were brewing in 2013, it is possible that none of the tragic developments that took place in Ukraine during and after the Maidan could have happened if not for the intrusion of foreign powers. Russia supported Donbas rebels after the overturning of power in Kyiv, while the United States had been deeply involved in staging the Euromaidan coup d'état in the first place. For many critical observers, it was obvious that this unconditional U.S.-led support for the overthrowing of the Kyiv government amounted to an "American-led effort to make Ukraine a western bulwark on Russia's borders," in the words of John Mearsheimer (2022, 31:08–31:15). The strategy included Ukraine's integration into the EU and—most importantly—its incorporation into NATO. The latter has been "the brightest of all red lines" for the Kremlin (Mearsheimer, 2022, 33:18–33:21).

The president of Russia repeatedly highlighted that a NATO expansion to Russia's borders would be an existential threat.

In the mainstream representation of the Ukrainian crisis by U.S. politicians and media, however, Putin's opposition to Ukraine becoming an "anti-Russia," as he called it, did not come across as a legitimate security concern; the mainstream Western discourse presented it as the "imperial ambition" of a dangerous dictator willing to trample on Ukraine's independence, democracy, and civilizational aspirations (Boyd-Barrett, 2017; 2020). The employment of this rhetoric allowed the United States not only to blame Moscow for the outbreak of the Ukrainian crisis but also to present itself as Ukraine's defender and savior.

"I hope that the people of Ukraine know that the United States stands with you . . . for the European future you have chosen and deserve"—this is how Victoria Nuland, the U.S. assistant secretary of state during the Euromaidan, addressed those gathered in the center of Kyiv (Azattyk, 2013, 0:13–20:32). Nuland distributed food among the pro-Maidan protesters, a highly symbolic gesture whose meaning could hardly be called subtle. It acquired even more symbolic value after December 2013, when Nuland publicly acknowledged that the United States had "invested over $5 billion to assist Ukraine" in building "democratic skills and institutions, as they promote civic participation and good governance, all of which are preconditions for Ukraine to achieve its European aspirations" (FailWin Compilation, 2014, 7:32–37:47). To spend five billion dollars to achieve a democratic condition in which half of the country is not considered—what kind of democracy is this and whose interests does it serve? This is what millions of Ukrainians who rejected or doubted the Euromaidan might have asked themselves.

The situation became even more obvious after the public release of a bugged phone conversation between Nuland and Geoffrey Pyatt, the then U.S. Ambassador to Ukraine, in which they discussed "which of the Ukrainian opposition figures ought to go into the government," revealing "how deeply the United States is enmeshed into internal Ukrainian affairs," as the *Nation* observed (Dreyfuss, 2014).

Clearly, Nuland's ostentatious support of the revolution was in line with the official White House position, which mirrored the Ukrainian narrative about the Euromaidan word for word. President Barack Obama defined the Maidan as a people's uprising for democracy, joined by courageous Ukrainian citizens from all parts of the country. "We saw in the Maidan how ordinary people from all parts of the country had said that we want a change," Obama (2014a) claimed, ignoring that half of the country did not support the revolution. In Obama's representation, those who opposed the Maidan and the new government were not a part of "the people of Ukraine"—they were "armed militias" (Obama, 2014b) and "Russian-backed separatists" (Obama, 2014c) who were trained, armed, and supported by Russia. In contrast to peace-loving and democracy-minded Ukrainians, who "reject[ed] violence," "reject[ed] corruption," and "reject[ed] that past" (Obama, 2014b), "Russian-backed separatists," in Obama's presentation, "violate[d] international law, violate[d] sovereignty, and ha[d] spurred great violence" (Obama, 2014b).

The arbitrariness of this juxtaposition is obvious for anybody who followed the development of the Euromaidan. Molotov cocktails, burned administrative buildings, wounded and mutilated policemen, tortured representatives of the "criminal" state, and humiliated opponents whose foreheads were marked with "slave" signs—all these could hardly support Obama's belief in "the principle of nonviolence" (Obama, 2014a) supposedly demonstrated by the Maidan supporters. However, this counterfactual hegemonic construction had an important strategic significance: It allowed the issue to be articulated in such a way that it appeared not to be a conflict within Ukraine, but between its alleged social unity and a threat to this unity from the outside—a threat to all Ukrainian people, unified under the state sovereignty of Ukraine. This, in turn, provided the United States an opportunity to intervene—to support Ukraine's "sovereignty" and the "democratic aspirations" of its "people" imagined in homogeneous terms.

The condition of possibility for the war of Ukraine against its own citizens was labeling the insurgents "pro-Russian separatists" and "terrorists" who had been serving Russia by fighting against the Maidan. For this condition to be met, not only the discourse of "civilization versus barbarism" but also "Ukraine's sovereignty versus Russia-backed separatism" needed to be stabilized and normalized. As always, an indispensable service in this sense has been provided by mainstream global media whose journalists did not incorporate the opinions of Ukrainians with alternative, anti-Maidan perspectives (Boyd-Barrett, 2017). Consumers of global media products had little chance to learn anything meaningful about the insurgency in Eastern Ukraine except that the rebels were "thugs, thieves, rapists, ex-cons, and vandals" (Lévy, 2014), "drunken separatists" (Black et al., 2014), and "barbarians" (Birnbaum & Morello, 2014). This one-dimensional vision of the Ukrainian crisis, established globally from its very onset, had tremendously significant consequences not only for the people of Donbas, who have been living in a state of war since 2014, but also for the whole of Ukraine, which in February 2022 was plunged into full-scale military conflict.

The Advent of the Comedian: Zelensky's Populism on the Fringes of the Virtual and the Real

The presidential victory of Volodymyr Zelensky—a former comedian with no political experience whatsoever—came as a result of people's fatigue with the war and with the "paranoid politics" of fear associated with the conflict, when "every day here is an agent of Moscow, an agent of the Kremlin, an agent of Russia, an agent of the FBI" (Karasyov, 2019, 15:00–15:06). According to Vadim Karasyov, director of the Kyiv-based Institute of Global Strategies, corrupted elites "switched paranoia on" to hold on to political power, while people wanted "to return to normal life and get out of this madhouse." Political decisions were thus driven by a widely shared longing for peace, national unity, and centrism (Karasyov, 2019, 16:20–18:50). In their desire for "normal life," most Ukrainians—73.2 percent of the popular vote in the second round of the presidential election in 2019—supported the vision put forward by Zelensky: A beautiful, bright, humorous dream world in which peace reigns and there is no splitting of the country into "right" and "wrong" Ukrainians.

The astonishing victory of Zelensky and his party Servant of the People, later transformed into a parliamentary machine to churn out and rubber-stamp neoliberal reforms (Baysha, 2022a), cannot be explained apart from the success of his television series *Servant of the People* (the party was named after it), which, as many observers believe, served as Zelensky's informal election platform. The main character of the series is Vasil Petrovych Holoborodko, a history teacher who wins the presidency in a landslide thanks to the support of ordinary Ukrainians, who crowdfund the necessary sum of money to register him as a "people's" presidential candidate.

The message delivered by Zelensky to Ukrainians through his show is clearly populist. To define the situation in Laclau's (2005) terms, *Servant of the People* draws a solid antagonistic frontier separating "the people" and "the elites." The equivalential chain of elements characterizing the latter includes stupidity, hypocrisy, venality, greed, unscrupulousness, gluttony, lust, and so forth. The country becomes healthy only after getting rid of both oligarchs and their puppets. Some of them are imprisoned or flee the country; their property is confiscated in an extrajudicial manner. In the show, Holoborodko publicly admits that he has "staged a coup in the country." "If I do something wrong," he says, addressing corrupted "others," "the people will tell me. But definitely not you" (*Servant of the People*, 2017, 22:42–22:48). In the clearest possible way, this excerpt illustrates the Manichean division of the Ukrainian social into two nonoverlapping entities: "good us," "the people," versus "bad them," corrupted elites.

Zelensky's pre-election speeches and interviews were so rare that they could have been counted on one's fingers; they were also light on policy specifics (Yaffa, 2019). The only way the people of Ukraine could get an idea of how Zelensky was planning to fix the country's problems was by watching his show. After all, he was not only an actor but also the co-owner of the studio producing it and co-author of the scripts, and for many observers, it was quite clear before the election that voters would take Holoborodko's promises as Zelensky's (Gordon, 2018b, 5:40–47:59). In other words, by means of Holoborodko—his virtual double—Zelensky was able to perform his populist election promises rather than just state them.

Most Ukrainians considered Zelensky a candidate of national unity and peace, even though his election platform contained very few policy specifics on the issues of war and peace (Zelensky, 2019). This is what the program states about the goal of ending the war:

> We must win peace for Ukraine. Before the guarantors of the Budapest Memorandum[10] and partners with the EU, we will raise the issue of supporting Ukraine in its efforts to end the war, return the temporarily occupied territories and force the aggressor to compensate for the damage caused. Surrender of national interests and territories cannot be subject to any negotiations.
>
> (Zelensky, 2019)

The platform does not explain how exactly Zelensky was planning to "win peace for Ukraine," "return the temporarily occupied territories," and "force the aggressor to compensate for the damage caused."

Zelensky's rare pre-election speeches and interviews were not helpful, either. I have managed to find only one interview, from 2018, in which Zelensky shared his thoughts on how peace could be achieved. Here is an excerpt:

Zelensky: The Minsk agreements [11] do not work, right? Right. To go there [Donbas and Crimea] by war? I am against this. . . . We will have to talk. We will. Whether we want it or not . . . I am ready to negotiate with the bald devil [12] not to allow a single person to die.

Host: Do you imagine yourself negotiating with the bald devil?

Zelensky: Easily. Why not? . . . It is necessary to speak in very simple terms. What do you want? Your goal? Why have you come to us? What do you need, guys? Here are your points. Then, I would take these points—we need to promote our own terms—and then I would say: "Here are our points." Somewhere in the middle we would agree.

Host: This means that something would have to be given up. . . . Could you explain this to people?

Zelensky: 100%. I'd say, "Folks, I talked to him, here's the list. And here is our list. And here is what they will go for. . . . I believe that it should be this way. But. Like the presidential election, it's all up to you." (Gordon, 2018a, 32:14–34:45)

To finalize the process, Zelensky suggested a national referendum, or—if there were difficulties in organizing such a vote due to the opposition—to gauge the people's will using the Internet or TV. "The list is approved—here we go"—such was Zelensky's peace plan (Gordon, 2018a, 35:10–35:13).

Even without close inspection, all the premises on which Zelensky grounded the possibility of establishing peace seem problematic. First, from Putin's point of view, it was Ukraine that did not fulfill the Minsk agreements—not that the pacts simply "did not work" by themselves, as Zelensky implied.

It was rather optimistic, therefore, to expect Putin to meet with Zelensky to renegotiate the agreement whose non-implementation, in his view, was Ukraine's fault. Even less likely was the prospect of a breakthrough by way of a heart-to-heart discussion as suggested by Zelensky—after all, since 2015, when the Minsk agreements were signed, much ink had been spent analyzing the benefits of the agreements for Moscow and the reasons it insisted on full implementation (see Chapter 6). Finally, it was not at all predetermined, given the rise of radicalism in Ukraine, that most Ukrainians would approve any version of territorial compromise between Kyiv and Moscow. In other words, Zelensky's "peace plan" did not seem to be a working plan at all. Rather, it looked like what Ruth Wodak (2003) calls "calculated ambivalence"—a populist strategy of presenting controversial issues "in a way that allows for possible ambiguous interpretations and is open for at least two opposite meanings" (p. 142).

Regarding Zelensky's populism and the calculated ambivalence in his discussions of most complex societal issues, it is noteworthy that his show *Servant of the People*—his unofficial campaign platform—ignored the theme of the Donbas war, which erupted in 2014, a year before the series started being broadcast. As the Maidan and Russia–Ukraine relations were very divisive issues in Ukrainian society, Zelensky simply ignored them so as not to jeopardize the unity of the nation to which he appealed—his viewers and, ultimately, his voters.

The calculated ambivalence employed by Zelensky turned out to be successful. Ukrainians voted for the comedian, swayed by his evasive promise to achieve peace and return Ukraine to normal. Unsurprisingly—given the quality of his plan—peace and normalcy were not delivered. As a matter of fact, little of what had been promised by Zelensky-Holoborodko to "make the teacher live as the president, and the president live as the teacher" (*Servant of the People*, 2016, 13:00–13:04) was fulfilled. In contrast, the unpopular neoliberal reforms he went on to initiate only worsened the standard of living for Ukrainians (Baysha, 2022a).

The reality of Zelensky's presidency—his forcing through of unpopular reforms, combined with the ongoing war in Donbas that he promised to stop, the lack of criminal cases against corrupt officials and oligarchs whom he promised to imprison, as well as industrial decline, salaries in arrears, budget shortfalls, rising unemployment and catastrophic rates of labor migration and depopulation, plus various scandals inside his party—led to massive levels of discontent. In January 2022, one month before the war, sociological data showed that 64.7 percent of Ukrainians believed the country was "moving in the wrong direction"; Zelensky's presidential approval rating was as low as 17 percent (KIIS, 2022). It was Russia's SMO, launched in February 2022, that transformed Zelensky from an unpopular ruler selling Ukrainian land against the people's will (Baysha, 2022b) into a transnational hero struggling against tyranny and barbarism.

Notes

1 This agreement was an extension of the European Neighborhood Policy (ENP) project launched by the EU in 2004 with an idea of creating a comfort zone around the Union—a "ring of friends" that would be aligned with the West though without necessarily becoming EU members.

2 "Svoboda," organized in 1991, was initially called the "Social-National Party of Ukraine" (SNPU). In 2000, SNPU changed its name to "Svoboda" ("freedom" in Ukrainian) and its official symbol was switched from a neo-Nazi Wolfsangel to a trident (the emblem of Ukraine). "Svoboda" is well-known for anti-Semitic public speeches by its leaders.

3 On December 2, 2013, the day after the storming of the governmental district, the Ministry of Internal Affairs of Ukraine reported that 140 police officers sought medical attention; 75 of them were hospitalized, with five in critical condition (Ukrainska Pravda, 2013).

4 "Sovok"/"sovki" is a derogatory term to denote the Soviet Union and the mental condition of those nostalgic for it.

5 A "vatnik" is a cotton-padded coat popular in the rural areas of Russia. Because, in the eyes of the supporters of the Maidan, its opponents were crude, unsophisticated, pro-Russian peasants, they came to be called "vatniki" (Baysha, 2020a, 2020b).

6 On January 16, 2014, the Ukrainian Parliament passed so-called dictatorship laws stating that wearing helmets in public was illegal. To protest these restrictions, some participants of the Maidan covered their heads with cookware instead of helmets. In the eyes of Maidan opponents, the performance came to signify a brainless condition or hollow idiocy, as suggested by the use of "kastrulegoloviye" (panhead) as an insult.

7 "Maidown" ("maidauni" in plural) is a compound word uniting "Maidan" and "Down," as in Down syndrome; it has been used to ascribe Maidan support to an "abnormal" mental condition.

8 Referring to Maidan participants as "skakuni" (jumpers) traces back to late November 2013, when students protesting on the Maidan created an action of jumping while chanting, "If you are not jumping, you are a Moskal [a derogatory term for Russians]" (Radio Liberty, 2013). Labeled as "skakuni," the protesters were cast as childish or infantile.

9 Igor Girkin, whose nickname is Strelkov, is a former officer of the Federal Security Service (FSB) of Russia, who was an active participant in the Donbas uprising; on May 16, 2014, he assumed the post of the Minister of Defense of the Donetsk People's Republic (DPR), which by that time had announced its independence from Ukraine.

10 The Budapest Memorandum, signed on December 5, 1994, prohibited the Russian Federation, the United Kingdom, and the United States from using military force against Ukraine in exchange for Ukraine giving up its nuclear weapons.

11 The Minsk agreements were a series of international agreements which sought to end the Donbas war. Minsk I was signed on September 5, 2014 and Minsk II on February 12, 2015. Both were made possible by decisive routs of the Ukrainian army—in the battles of Ilovaisk and Debaltseve, respectively. More on this in Chapter 6.

12 Zelensky uses the phrase "bald devil" as part of an idiomatic expression that suggests readiness to make a bargain with anybody to achieve one's goals. In an apparent double entendre, the epithet is here taken as a reference to the balding Russian president.

Reference List

Áslund, A. (2015). *Ukraine: What went wrong and how to fix it.* Peterson Institute for International Economics.

Azattyk. (2013, December 11). Nuland: A European future for Ukraine is still possible. *YouTube.* www.youtube.com/watch?v=znXpmeV2y8M

Baysha, O. (2015). Ukrainian Euromaidan: The exclusion of otherness in the name of progress. *European Journal of Cultural Studies, 18*(1), 3–18. doi:10.1177/1367549414557806.

Baysha, O. (2016). European integration as imagined by Ukrainian Pravda bloggers. In M. Pantti (Ed.), *Media and the Ukraine crisis: Hybrid media practices and narratives of conflict* (pp. 71–88). Peter Lang.

Baysha, O. (2017). In the name of national security: Articulating ethnopolitical struggles as terrorism. *Journal of Multicultural Discourses, 14*(4), 332–348. doi:10.1080/17447143.2017.1363217.

Baysha, O. (2018). *Miscommunicating social change: Lessons from Russia and Ukraine.* Lexington.

Baysha, O. (2020a). Dehumanizing political others: A discursive-material perspective. *Critical Discourse Studies, 17*(3), 292–307. doi:10.1080/17405904.2019.1567364

Baysha, O. (2020b). The antagonistic discourses of the Euromaidan: Koloradi, sovki, and vatniki vs. jumpers, maidowns, and panheads. In N. Knoblock (Ed.), *Language of conflict: Discourses of the Ukrainian crisis* (pp. 101–117). Bloomsbury Academic.

Baysha, O. (2020c). The impossible totality of Ukraine's "people": On the populist discourse of the Ukrainian Maidan. In M. Kranert (Ed.), *Discursive approaches to populism across disciplines* (pp. 63–90). Palgrave Macmillan.

Baysha, O. (2022a). *Democracy, populism, and neoliberalism in Ukraine: On the fringes of the virtual and the real.* Routledge.

Baysha, O. (2022b). On the impossibility of discursive-material closures: A case of banned TV channels in Ukraine. *Social Sciences & Humanities Open, 6*(1), 100329. doi:10.1016/j.ssaho.2022.100329

Birnbaum, M., & Morello, C. (2014, July 22). Train leaves Ukraine war zone with victims of Malaysia plane, black boxed handed. *Washington Post.* www.washingtonpost.com/world/2014/07/21/86cd2a12-10b0-11e4-98ee-daea85133bc9_story.html

Black, P., Shoichet, C., & Almasy, S. (2014, July 24). Kerry on MH17: "Drunken separatists" interfering at MH17 crash site. *CNN.* https://edition.cnn.com/2014/07/20/world/europe/ukraine-malaysia-airlines-crash/index.html

Boyd-Barrett, J. O. (2017). Ukraine, mainstream media and conflict propaganda. *Journalism Studies, 18*(8), 1016–1034. doi:10.1080/1461670X.2015.1099461

Boyd-Barrett, J. O. (2020). *Russiagate and propaganda: Disinformation in the age of social media.* Routledge.

Bistritsky, Y. (2013, November 29). You believed ridiculous words (in Ukrainian). *Ukrainska Pravda.* www.pravda.com.uacolumns/2013/12/18/7007461

Crisis Group. (2022). *Conflict in Ukraine's Donbass.* www.crisisgroup.org/content/conflict-ukraines-donbas-visual-explainer

Dreyfuss, B. (2014, February 10). The not-so-secret Ukraine phone call. *Nation.* www.thenation.com/article/not-so-secret-ukraine-phone-call

Dubrovsky, V. (2013, December 21). Shame and fear (in Ukrainian). *Ukrainska Pravda.* www.pravda.com.ua/columns/2013/12/21/7007945

FailWin Compilation. (2014, February 9). Victoria Nuland admits Washington has spent $5 billion to "subvert Ukraine." *YouTube*. www.youtube.com/watch? v=U2fYcHLouXY

Farion, I. (2014, December 20). Iryna Farion's speech at the Maidan of Independence (in Ukrainian). *YouTube*. www.youtube.com/watch?v=-QOdRudKVk

Gordon, D. (2014a). *In Lugansk, separatists occupied the department of the national security service* (in Russian). http://gordonua.com/news/society/v-luganske-separatisty-zahvatili-upravlenie-sbu-17118.html

Gordon, D. (2014b). *Two meetings are held in Kharkov: One for federalization, another for the unity of Ukraine* (in Russian). http://m.gordonua.com/news/maidan/v--harkove-prohodit-dva-mitinga-za-federalizaciyu-iza-edinstvo-ukrainy-16017.html

Gordon, D. (2018a, December 25). Visiting Dmytro Gordon, part 2 (in Russian). *YouTube*. www.youtube.com/watch?v=fwuOfFlLn88

Gordon, D. (2018b, December 25). Visiting Dmytro Gordon, part 3 (in Russian). *YouTube*. www.youtube.com/watch?v=VPE2hv8qbBc&t=725s

Hrytsenko, A. (2013, December 15). Two different Ukraines (in Ukrainian). *Ukrainska Pravda*. http://blogs.pravda.com.ua/authors/grytsenko/52ae1bbb1e26e

Karasyov, V. (2019, April 10). Vadim Karasyov on 112 (in Russian). *YouTube*. www. youtube.com/watch?v=L6g443XgNPw

Katchanovski, I. (2016). The Maidan massacre in Ukraine: A summary of analysis, evidence and findings. In J. L. Black & M. Johns (Eds.), *The return of the cold war: Ukraine, the West and Russia* (pp. 220–4). Routledge.

KIIS. (2014, April 20). The views and opinions of south-eastern regions residents of Ukraine. *Kyiv International Institute of Sociology*. www.kiis.com.ua/?lang=eng&cat =reports&id=302&y=2014&page=9

KIIS. (2015, October 7). What path of integration should Ukraine choose. *Kyiv International Institute of Sociology*. https://kiis.com.ua/?lang=eng&cat=reports&id=556

KIIS. (2022, January 24). Socio-political moods of the population of Ukraine. *Kyiv International Institute of Sociology*. www.kiis.com.ua/?lang=eng&cat=reports&id= 1090&page=1

Kull, S. (2015, March 9). The Ukrainian people on the current crisis. *Program for Public Consultation/Kiev International Institute of Sociology*. https://publicconsultation. org/wp-content/uploads/2016/03/Ukraine_0315.pdf

Kush, L. (2014, January 24). What the residents of Donbass and Crimea think about the Maidan (in Russian). *BBC*. www.bbc.com/russian/international/2014/01/140121_ ukraine_regions_mood.

Kuzio, T. (2017). *Putin's war against Ukraine: Revolution, nationalism, and crime*. CreateSpace Independent Publishing Platform.

Laclau, E. (2005). *On populist reason*. Verso.

Leviy Bereg. (2014, April 7). *In Nikolaev, separatists try to storm the building of the regional state administration*. http://lb.ua/society/2014/04/07/262274_nikolaeve_ separatisti_pitayutsya.html

Lévy, B. (2014, July 22). Putin's crime, Europe's cowardice. *New York Times*. www. nytimes.com/2014/07/23/opinion/putins-crime-europes-cowardice.html

Lutsenko, Y. (2013, December 13). Yuri Lutsenko's speech at the Maidan podium. *YouTube*. www.youtube.com/watch?v=kynOMmtDl3c

Matveeva, A. (2022). Donbas: The post-Soviet conflict that changed Europe. *European Politics and Society*, *23*(3), 410–441. doi:10.1080/23745118.2022.2074398

Mearsheimer, J. (2022, June 16). The causes and consequences of the Ukraine war. *YouTube*. www.youtube.com/watch?v=qciVozNtCDM&t=750s

Obama, B. (2014a, March 12). Remarks by President Obama and Ukraine Prime Minister Yatsenyuk after bilateral meeting. *White House Press Release*. www.whitehouse.gov/the-press-office/2014/03/12/remarks-president-obama-and-ukraine-primeminister-yatsenyuk-after-bilat

Obama, B. (2014b, June 4). Remarks by President Obama and President-Elect Petro Poroshenko of Ukraine after bilateral meeting. *White House Press Release*. www.whitehouse.gov/the-press-office/2014/06/04/remarks-president-obama-and-president-elect-petro-poroshenko-ukraine-aft

Obama, B. (2014c, July 18). Statement by the president on Ukraine. *White House Press Release*. www.whitehouse.gov/the-press-office/2014/07/18/statement-presidentukraine

Petro, N. (2022). *The tragedy of Ukraine*. De Gruyter.

Radio Liberty. (2013, December 4). *From Maidan to Berkut: A Ukraine protest glossary*. www.rferl.org/a/ukraine-protest-glossary-uromaydan/25190085.html

Sakwa, R. (2015). *Frontline Ukraine: Crisis in borderlands*. I. B. Tauris.

Servant of the People. (2016, June 2). Season 1, episodes 1–4. *YouTube*. www.youtube.com/watch?v=_DXc_KyXdiU=790s

Servant of the People. (2017, November 2). Season 2, episode 16. *YouTube*. www.youtube.com/watch?v=JyIdyVH00P8

Sinchenko, D. (2014, February 10). The front line (in Ukrainian). *Ukrainska Pravda*. www.pravda.com.ua/columns/2014/02/10/7013300

Slovoidilo. (2021, August 24). *30 years of independence: How the attitude of Ukrainians towards NATO has been changing*. www.slovoidilo.ua/2021/08/24/infografika/suspilstvo/30-rokiv-nezalezhnosti-yak-zminyuvalosya-stavlennya-ukrayincziv-chlenstva-nato

Turchynov, O. (2014). The statement by Turchynov on the situation in the southeast of Ukraine. *YouTube*. www.youtube.com/watch?v=aLjrsQpcRX4

Ukrainska Pravda. (2013, December 2). *Police reported 75 of its servicemen had been hospitalized* (in Ukrainian). www.pravda.com.ua/news/2013/12/2/7004254/

Ukrainska Pravda. (2014a). *In Kharkiv, separatists demand a referendum on the federalization of Ukraine* (in Ukrainian). www.pravda.com.ua/news/2014/03/16/7019010

Ukrainska Pravda. (2014b). *Yatsenyuk: In the east, a plan of invading Ukraine is implemented* (in Ukrainian). www.pravda.com.ua/news/2014/04/7/7021563

UN OHCHR. (2017, December 12). *Report on the human rights situation in Ukraine*. Office of the United Nations High Commissioner for Human Rights. www.ohchr.org/Documents/Countries/UA/UAReport20th_EN.pdf

Wilson, A. (2014). *Ukraine crisis: What it means for the West*. Yale University Press.

Wodak, R. (2003). Populist discourses: The rhetoric of exclusion in written genres. *Document Design*, *4*(2), 132–148. doi:10.1075/dd.4.2.04wod

Yaffa, J. (2019, October 25). Ukraine's unlikely president, promising a new style of politics, gets a taste of Trump's swamp. *New Yorker*. www.newyorker.com/magazine/2019/11/04/how-trumps-emissaries-put-pressure-on-ukraines-new-president

Zelensky, V. (2019). *Election platform of the presidential candidate Volodymyr Zelensky* (in Ukrainian). https://program.ze2019.com/

2 Analyzing Populist Discourses

Contingency, Sedimentation, and Antagonism

Discourse Theory of Laclau and Mouffe

The research presented in this book draws on the discourse theory (DT) of Ernesto Laclau and Chantal Mouffe, according to which social objectivity is only possible on the condition of "discursivity," where "discourse" is understood as a "social fabric" on which "social actors occupy differential positions" (Laclau & Mouffe, 1985, p. xiii). It appears to be a "force which contributes to the moulding and constitution of social relations" (Laclau & Mouffe, 1985, p. 110). Discourse is conceptualized as a "structured totality resulting from the articulatory practice," where "articulation" means "any practice establishing relations among elements" of the discursive field—a reservoir of all available signs (Laclau & Mouffe, 1985, p. 105). Discourses are stabilized by nodal points or "master-signifiers," which assume "a 'universal' structuring function" (Laclau & Mouffe, 1985, p. 98).

A discourse forms when elements from the discursive field are articulated through being equivalentially linked to one another: They acquire their meanings only in conjunction with other elements of the chain. Through articulation, elements become fixed as "moments of a stable articulatory structure" (Laclau & Mouffe, 1985, p. 96). If used by alternative discourses, the same signifiers may come to be linked to alternative chains of equivalence. If this happens, such a signifier becomes "floating" once again; its meaning appears to be "suspended" across different structures of signification.

All the basic nodal points discussed in this book—the (Euro)Maidan, the ATO, the SMO, the Minsk agreements, and so forth—appear to be floating signifiers, because they are linked to entirely different associations within the opposing discourses endorsed by Zelensky and journalists/bloggers propagating alternative views. In other words, in different discourses, these nodal points have different meanings, which are not pre-given. They emerge through articulatory practices as "attempts to dominate the field of discursivity, to arrest the flow of differences, to construct a center" (Laclau & Mouffe, 1985, p. 112). However, no ultimate fixation of meaning is possible since any discursive totality is "subverted by a field of discursivity which overflows

DOI: 10.4324/9781003379164-4

it" (Laclau & Mouffe, 1985, p. 113). In the case under consideration, this is well illustrated by the fact that, despite all attempts to shut down oppositional articulations, the post-Maidan Ukrainian state has not been able to silence the opposition completely, as its discourse has continued to reemerge in new discursive-material configurations.

The paradoxical impossibility yet necessity of discursive closures is one of the central points in DT. On the one hand, no signification is possible without discursive closures; on the other hand, such closures are always precarious and unstable. Any ultimate fixing of meanings is inconceivable given that they can be destabilized at any time through the activation of alternative links between the elements of the discursivity field. It is here that the idea of contingency, central to DT, comes to the fore. Because signs may be linked to alternative associations, which may lead to the formation of alternative discourses, any meaning and any social configuration (as DT equates the social and the discursive) are seen as subject to change.

Although no ultimate fixing of meaning is possible, prolonged (though finite) discursive closures do happen—either through social "sedimentation" when "the system of possible alternatives tends to vanish and the traces of the original contingency to fade" (Laclau, 1990, p. 34) or through "administrative practices which deal bureaucratically with social issues" (Laclau, 2001, p. 12). The latter is central to this research. By banning oppositional media and prosecuting oppositional journalists/bloggers, Ukraine's post-Maidan regime has been striving to stabilize meanings favorable to its political course, taking away their precarity and instability so as to make them immutable and fixed. The sedimentation of these meanings occurred when, as a result of the "cleaning up" of the information space from alternative interpretations, these meanings came to be normalized to the point of common sense.

As I show in the second part of the book, to achieve this level of normalization, the post-Maidan regime had to transform discursively the oppositional media into enemies of the people, as well as liquidate them physically by shutting down their broadcasting operations and subjecting journalists to arrests, forced exile, or even murder (see Chapter 4). In other words, the Ukrainian state had to disable the discursive-material assemblages behind the production of oppositional interpretations. One cannot fully grasp the situation without accounting for the interrelation of its material and discursive aspects—an analytical enterprise in which Carpentier's (2017) discursive-material knot (DMK) will be a useful analytical tool.

In Carpentier's (2017) view, which he builds on Laclau and Mouffe's insight about discourse being formed through the interplay of both "linguistic and non-linguistic elements" (Laclau & Mouffe, 1985, p. 108), the expansion of discourse theory to include the material makes analysis of the social richer, while also allowing otherwise invisible forces to be recognized, adding contingency to established meanings. As Carpentier (2017) puts it, the incorporation of the material into analysis "shows a richer landscape of forces that can destabilize existing sedimentations, and create more contingency" (p. 68). The increased contingency of all the DMK components works against discursive closures, thereby boosting the likelihood of established/hegemonic meanings being challenged.

By the logic of invitation and dislocation, the material participates in discursive struggles over meanings, suggesting this or that particular articulation. Objects enter the social not only by assuming the role of intermediaries or mediators but also by acting as social agents of their own. Any event—any material change—can dislocate discourse if the latter proves unable to attribute meaning to the former; in such cases, the material destabilizes discourses by pointing to their internal contradictions and their limited capacity to represent the material world. The material can disrupt or strengthen discursive orders; however, it is also possible that its invitation could be ignored, and an alternative meaning attached to it. Carpentier's (2017) model thus allows seeing meanings/social configurations as even more contingent; it provides an opportunity to understand social change through the shifting landscape of discursive-material configurations.

Theory of Populism by Laclau

In my analysis of Zelensky's populism, I also draw on the theory of populism by Ernesto Laclau, which he developed based on the discourse theory elaborated in partnership with Mouffe (Laclau, 2000; 2005; 2014). In Laclau's theorizing, populism appears not as an ideology or "a type of movement—identifiable with either a special social base or a particular ideological orientation—but a political logic" (Laclau, 2005, p. 117). It is a "way of constituting the very unity of the group," "the people" (Laclau, 2005, p. 74). According to Laclau, "the people" of a populist movement appear when one unsatisfied democratic demand—the smallest unit of his analysis—comes to be united with other demands, and when these demands are "equivalently" united to oppose the established order.[1] This chain of otherwise different and sometimes even incommensurable claims is equivalent only in one sense: vis-à-vis the "otherness" of those excluded from the newly established populist collective/totality. The exclusion of "otherness" is thus the condition that sets up the emergence of "the people," and thereby enables populism to take root: "To grasp that totality conceptually, we have to grasp its limits—that is to say, we have to differentiate it from something other than itself" (Laclau, 2005, p. 69). Therefore, the simplification of the social and its Manichean division into "us" versus "them" are the most readily distinguishable features of populism.

Any populist identity for "the people," created through the equivalential chaining of various unsatisfied demands, will necessarily be full of internal contradictions and tensions, as the constructed external equivalence always subverts internal differences. Accordingly, all populist identities are formed through the tension of differential and equivalential logics. "What we have ultimately," Laclau (2005) claims,

> is a failed totality, the place of an irretrievable fullness. This totality is an object which is both impossible and necessary. Impossible, because the tension between equivalence and difference is ultimately insurmountable; necessary, because without some kind of closure, however precarious it might be, there would be no signification and no identity.
>
> (p. 70)

Any "closure," in turn, requires naming, which is essential in constituting the unity of a populist collective: It serves as "a social cement" (Laclau, 2005, p. x) used to assemble the heterogeneous elements of the impossible but necessary unity. Without naming, the collective cannot be formed; it comes into existence through signification, when one particularity (democratic demand), "without ceasing to be a particular difference, assumes the representation of an incommensurable totality" (Laclau, 2005, p. 70). To go beyond a vague feeling of solidarity and form "the people" of populism, equivalential relations need to be crystallized "in a certain discursive identity which no longer represents democratic demands as equivalent, but the equivalential link as such" (Laclau, 2005, p. 93).

According to Laclau (2005), the newly established populist identity "becomes something of the order of an empty signifier, its own particularity embodying an unachievable fullness" (p. 71). Representing the ever-larger chain of demands, it "has to dispossess itself of particularistic contents in order to embrace social demands which are quite heterogeneous" (Laclau, 2005, p. 96). In other words, the "emptiness" of the signifiers that provide unity and identity to a popular camp is not the result of ideological or political underdevelopment; rather, it is a structural necessity. The wider the equivalential chain, the more difficult it is to determine the identity of the populist collective in any clear terms: "It is here that the moment of emptiness necessarily arises. . . . Ergo, 'vagueness' and 'imprecision', but these do not result from any kind of marginal or primitive situation; they are inscribed in the very nature of the political" (Laclau, 2005, pp. 98–99). The language of a populist discourse, therefore, regardless of its ideological leaning, will always be "imprecise and fluctuating: not because of any cognitive failure, but because it tries to operate performatively within a social reality which is to a large extent heterogeneous and fluctuating" (Laclau, 2005, p. 118).

Because any assemblage of heterogeneous elements can only be kept together if unified by a single name, and because "the extreme form of singularity is an individuality" (Laclau, 2005, p. 100), the group is often identified with the name of its leader. The whole process of "investing" one signifier with the meaning of "mythical fullness" is unthinkable without "affect"—the moment of "enjoyment" (Laclau, 2005, pp. 111–115). "There is no populism," Laclau claims, "without affective investment in a partial object" (2005, p. 116); "pure harmony would be incompatible with affect" (2005, p. 118). When a "popular demand" appears—passionately formed from the plurality of unsatisfied social claims—an internal antagonistic frontier emerges, separating the institutionalized system from the people. The social is dichotomized. This division is sustained through the employment of privileged signifiers like "regime" or "oligarchy" to denote the totality of the "evil other" as well as "the people" or "the nation" to denote the "good us."

According to Laclau, the emergence of an antagonistic frontier is an essential feature of populism. However, things become far more complex as this dichotomizing frontier persists after the equivalential chain of the popular camp is interrupted "by an alternative equivalential chain, in which some of the popular demands are articulated to entirely different links" (Laclau, 2005, p. 131). If this is the case, the meanings of the demands become "indeterminate between alternative equivalential frontiers" (Laclau, 2005, p. 131). A signifier whose meaning is "suspended" in this way is called "floating"; it is used to organize alternative discourses and alternative ways of constructing "the people," until the outcome of the hegemonic struggle determines which meaning will ultimately be fixed.

It is the unending, undecidable game between the "empty" and the "floating" that constitutes the essence of the "political," whose "operation par excellence is always going to be the construction of a 'people'" (Laclau, 2005, p. 153). In other words, according to Laclau, any political intervention is populistic to some extent, which "does not mean, however, that all political projects are equally populistic; that depends on the extension of the equivalential chain unifying social demands" (Laclau, 2005, p. 154). The more extended the chain, the more populist its discourse. According to Laclau,

We have two ways of constructing the social: either through the assertion of a particularity—in our case, a particularity of demands whose only links to other particularities are of a differential nature (as we have seen: no positive terms, only differences); or through a partial surrender of particularity, stressing what all particularities have, equivalentially, in common. The second mode of construction of the social involves, as we know, the drawing of an antagonistic frontier; the first does not. I have called the first mode of constructing the social logic of difference, and the second, logic of equivalence. Apparently, we could draw the conclusion that one precondition for the emergence of populism is the expansion of the equivalential logic at the expense of the differential one.

(Laclau, 2005, pp. 77–78)

Laclau acknowledges that in practice equivalence and difference are not mutually exclusive; they require each other for the construction of the social, which is characterized by this irreducible tension: "All social (that is discursive) identity is constructed at the meeting point of difference and equivalence" (Laclau, 2005, p. 80). However, "an institutionalist discourse is one that attempts to make the limits of the discursive formation coincide with the limits of the community," while in the case of populism, "the 'people' . . . is something less than the totality of the members of the community: it is a partial component which nevertheless aspires to be conceived as the only legitimate totality" (Laclau, 2005, p. 81).

The crux of the difference between an "institutional" discourse and a populist one is that the latter privileges some hegemonic (or empty) signifiers "which structure, as nodal points, the ensemble of a discursive formation" (Laclau, 2005, p. 81). It is these privileged signs that delimit the boundaries of the social constructed through populist equivalential logic. As Laclau puts it, "In order to have the 'people' of populism, we need . . . a plebs who claims to be the only legitimate populous—that is, a partiality which wants to function as the totality of the community" (2005, p. 81). In contrast, "institutional discourse" enables all differences to be considered as equally valid.

Theory of Antagonistic Discourse by Nico Carpentier

Finally, in my analysis of Zelensky's articulations, I refer to Nico Carpentier's (2017) theory of antagonistic discourse, which he developed while drawing on, among other theories, the ideas of Mouffe (2005, 2009, 2013) who emphasizes the importance of democracy of "a vibrant clash of democratic political positions" (2009, p. 104). Mouffe warns against what she calls the "closure of the democratic space" (2009, p. 77) and advocates for its radical openness. "One should realize," Mouffe (2009) argues, "that a lack of democratic contestation over real political alternatives leads to antagonisms manifesting themselves under forms that undermine the very basis of the democratic public sphere" (pp. 114–115). In contrast, a radical openness of democratic space would lead to recognizing unknown or suppressed possibilities, such as the existence of "other just political forms of society" (Mouffe, 2005, p. 62).

In Mouffe's view, the relations between the members of a community become more democratic when they acknowledge and accept the particularity and limitations of their claims. Since drawing frontiers of "us" versus "them" is necessary for identity construction, some frontiers/discursive closures are unavoidable; it is crucial to acknowledge, however, that all the moments of closure required for constituting such identifications can be negotiated in a variety of ways. The conflict between inclusion and exclusion (who belongs to "us" and "them") is permanent, and "no final resolution or equilibrium between those two conflicting logics is ever possible, and there can be only temporary, pragmatic, unstable and precarious negotiations of the tension between them" (Mouffe, 2009, p. 45).

According to Mouffe (2009), the stabilization of closures through the establishment of solid dividing frontiers leads to "antagonism proper—which takes place between enemies" (p. 13) and brings out totalitarian tendencies in government. This may happen when the frontiers are presented not as contingent and temporary, but as essential and natural—dictated by considerations of rationality or morality, for example. Without a plurality of competing forces attempting to define the common good differently, pluralistic democracy is impossible; instead, to achieve a democratic condition, a break with the tradition of universalization and homogenization of both the other and the self is required.

Since the political process is inconceivable without antagonism, which can never be eliminated, Mouffe (2009) claims, one of the major tasks of democratic politics is to transform antagonism into agonism. She describes agonism as a different mode for antagonism to manifest, because it involves a relationship not between enemies but between "adversaries," defined in a paradoxical way as "friendly enemies"—people who are friends because they share a common symbolic space, but also enemies because they want to organize this common symbolic space in different ways (Mouffe, 2009, p. 12).

The necessity of such a transformation stems from the acceptance of pluralism as a foundational principle of modern liberal democracy, understood not merely as a form of government but as a form of organizing human coexistence in political terms. According to this vision, difference (in views or subject positions) acquires a positive status: It should not be suppressed, but rather acknowledged and greeted as a condition that makes radical democratic projects possible.

Developing the ideas of Mouffe and other authors, Carpentier (2017) identifies three nodal points that, in his view, constitute antagonistic discourse: (1) the need for destruction of the enemy, (2) the radical difference of the enemy, and (3) homogenization of the self in opposition to the enemy (172). The radical difference between self and enemy, as presupposed by antagonistic discourse, appears when there is no symbolic space that the self and other can be imagined to share, as the two are thought to be irreconcilably at odds. As Carpentier (2017) puts it,

> The construction of this radical other is supported by the logic of dichotomy, whereas the idea of the absence of a common space produces distance. In the more extreme cases, this radical othering leads to a dehumanization and demonization of the other, denying even the most basic features of humanity to that other, which makes its destruction easier and even necessary.
>
> (p. 172)

Homogenization, another nodal point of antagonistic discourse, manifests itself in the solidification of the chain of equivalence among those united in their struggle against the common enemy (Carpentier, 2017, p. 173). In other words, the diversity within conflicting camps is obliterated to the extent that anybody who dares problematize total homogenization is branded a "traitor." This is what is often referred to as a "Jacobin imaginary," juxtaposing the imagined homogeneity of "us" against "them."

According to Carpentier (2017), to transform antagonism into agonism— that is, to stop seeing opponents as enemies and instead begin seeing them as adversaries (friendly enemies, to put in in Mouffe's (2005) terms)—it is nec- essary to rearticulate the nodal points of antagonistic discourse and recreate a common symbolic space among the conflicting participants in a political pro- cess. To re-establish "conflictual togetherness," as Carpentier (2017, p. 178) puts it, a structural balance needs to be restored so that the involved actors are no longer positioned hierarchically.

It is also necessary to move away from dichotomization, making the solid, impermeable frontiers between the self and the opponent more porous, in order to activate a diversity of positions and allow pluralism to flourish— a precondition for agonism to emerge. Introducing greater permeability between the identities of self and other as well as pluralizing the positions within each camp enables connections between former enemies, which can lead to alliances across borders and the creation of symbolic spaces of shar- ing. "If adversaries belong to the same political space, and do not attempt to destroy (or annihilate) each other, then a reflection on the nature of this interaction becomes unavoidable" (Carpentier, 2017, p. 179), paving the way to work out mutually acceptable terms of coexistence and reducing the chance of violence—physical, material, structural, or symbolic.

The transformation of antagonism into agonism is important for preserv- ing peace. This task requires establishing political mechanisms through which collective passions over the issue at stake are channeled and expressed with- out opponents being seen as enemies, but rather as "friendly adversaries." Pluralistic democracy presupposes a clash of different political positions and makes room for dissent; disagreement is considered legitimate and welcome. If this is missing, there is danger of replacing democratic contestation with violence, as happened in Ukraine during and after the Euromaidan, the tragic results of which we are seeing to this day.

Note

1 In Laclau's usage, "democratic demands" have nothing to do with a democratic regime, nor does the phrase imply any normative judgment; rather, it is strictly descriptive. What Laclau means is that these demands "are formulated to the system by an underdog of sorts" and "that their very emergence presupposes some kind of exclusion or deprivation" (Laclau, 2005, p. 125).

Reference List

Carpentier, N. (2017). *The discursive-material knot: Cyprus in conflict and community media participation.* Peter Lang.

Laclau, E. (1990). *New reflections on the revolution of our time.* Verso.

Laclau, E. (2000). Identity and hegemony: The role of universality in the constitution of political logics. In J. Butler, E. Laclau, & S. Žižek (Eds.), *Contingency, hegemony, universality: Contemporary dialogues on the left* (pp. 44–89). Verso.

Laclau, E. (2001). Democracy and the question of power. *Constellations, 8*(1), 3–14. doi:10.1111/1467-8675.00212

Laclau, E. (2005). *On populist reason.* Verso.

Laclau, E. (2014). *The rhetorical foundations of society.* Verso.

Laclau, E., & Mouffe, C. (1985). *Hegemony and socialist strategy: Towards a radical democratic politics.* Verso.

Mouffe, C. (2005). *On the political.* Routledge.

Mouffe, C. (2009). *The democratic paradox.* Verso.

Mouffe, C. (2013). *Agonistics: Thinking the world politically.* Verso.

3 Zelensky's Transnational Populism

"Civilized Us" Versus "Barbaric Them"

On February 24, 2022, Russia launched an attack on Ukraine, with Russia's official discourse calling it a "special military operation" while Kyiv labeled it "a full-fledged invasion of Ukraine," distinguishing this war from what had already been going on in Donbas. How did Zelensky present this new war to the global public? As my analysis of Zelensky's speeches and interviews shows, there have been three nodal points that stand out as the most important for Zelensky in sustaining the coherence of his discursive constructions. In all his speeches, Ukraine was presented as (1) an outpost of civilization, (2) a beacon of democracy, and (3) a unified social formation whose view of the ongoing crisis was shared by everyone but traitors/collaborators. In what follows, I will analyze these points one by one and discuss how Zelensky's transnational populism took shape around three privileged signifiers linked to Ukraine: civilization, democracy, and unity.

Civilized People of All Countries, Unite!

From the first days of Russia's SMO, the overarching frame of reference employed by Zelensky has been to cast the ongoing war as a story of barbarism/evil attacking civilization/good. "Nobody thought that in the modern world a human could act as a savage" (Zelensky, 2022c, 26:15–26:27)—such was his message to Western journalists on the tenth day of the war, with the reference to Russian troops. Russia's invasion, in many of Zelensky's speeches, appeared as "barbarism on a cosmic scale" (Zelensky, 2022ze, 4:30–34:33), while Russia itself was "total evil" (Zelensky, 2022g, 8:44–48:47). "Ukraine confronts barbarians. Inhumans," he informed the students and professors of UK universities (Zelensky, 2022zl, 2:43–52:49). Zelensky characterized Russians as "people of the Middle Ages" (Zelensky, 2022zx, 27:34–27:36), saying in his interview to NBC that Russians "do not even understand how civilization develops" (Zelensky, 2022zu, 23:10–23:12).

Zelensky constructed the war between Russia and Ukraine as his country's fight "against tyranny that wants to annihilate Europe and everything that

DOI: 10.4324/9781003379164-5

unites us" (Zelensky, 2022p, 5:11–15:18). "Russian occupiers bring tyranny, which does not allow for any freedom" (Zelensky, 2022zd, 2:32–34:40), he claimed while addressing the people of Iceland. "We are at war with Russia, but we are fighting for the values of the civilized world," he maintained in a discussion session for the *Wall Street Journal*'s CEO Council Summit (Zelensky, 2022zb, 28:28–34:41). "We must be an outpost of these values. . . . If not us, then who?" argued Zelensky while addressing Australia's Lowy Institute (Zelensky, 2022zzh, 15:43–16:00).

In a speech to Italy, Zelensky presented Ukraine as a "gateway to Europe," which "barbarians . . . want to break" (Zelensky, 2022j, 5:41–45:49). "Russia considers the territory of our state as a bridgehead for seizing the territories of other countries," he claimed while participating in a roundtable for the *Economist* (Zelensky, 2022zw, 9:10–19:20). "We are fighting today," Zelensky said in an address to the Polish Sejm, "so that such an evil time does not come for the Baltic countries and for Poland" (Zelensky, 2022d, 4:44–45:51). If Russia is not stopped, he asserted while speaking to the people of Belgium, "tyranny will come to take away from you what you possess and are proud of" (Zelensky, 2022p, 7:23–27:28). "To provide security for Ukraine means guaranteeing long-term security for Europe," he argued (Zelensky, 2022zw, 9:18–19:23). During his speech at the UN Security Council, Zelensky said, "Our independence is your security. The security of the entire free world" (Zelensky, 2022zzb, 10:12–10:16). "There is still a chance to stop tyranny on our land"—such was his message to the people of the people of the Netherlands (Zelensky, 2022q, 7:40–47:46).

Speaking at a meeting of the Joint Expeditionary Force, Zelensky called Russian troops "locusts" [саранча] that would inevitably invade Europe if Ukraine were to fall (Zelensky, 2022f, 12:43–12:44). "I'm sure you realize that if the Russian army is ordered to invade your land, they will do the same to your country," Zelensky told the politicians and people of Finland (Zelensky, 2022t, 5:28–35:39). In his address to South Korea, Zelensky argued that the goal of Russia's "barbaric state" was "to destroy first everything that makes us Ukrainians, a separate nation. . . . Then, to go further to Europe, then to Asia" (Zelensky, 2022u, 4:10–14:19). "Today the war is in Ukraine, but tomorrow it may be in Europe and the United States. Therefore, it is fair to say that the war in Ukraine is already a war in Europe and the USA," he maintained while communicating with NBC (Zelensky, 2022zu, 1:56–62:10).

As is evident from these excerpts, from the very first days of the war, Zelensky presented it as not just a conflict between Russia and Ukraine, but a larger clash between an uncivilized, savage Russia and the entire civilized world, including countries in Europe, North America, and Asia. As he put it in his interview for ZDF, "This is a war for all of us. And we can all win in it. . . . If we lose, it's not just Ukraine. All of Europe will lose" (Zelensky, 2022zzj, 4:41–44:50). Addressing the US Congress, Zelensky proclaimed that the purpose of the global anti-Russian coalition was not just to defend Ukraine, but to fight for the future of Europe and the whole planet: "We are fighting for the values of Europe, for the world, sacrificing our lives in the name of the future. . . . That's why today the American people are helping not just Ukraine but Europe and the world to keep the planet alive" (Zelensky, 2022h, 16:45–17:05).

Because Ukraine was fighting for the whole world, as Zelensky presented it, he could not condone neutrality with respect to the conflict. "We are civilized people. Therefore, I believe that the position of neutrality is out of date," he said to African journalists (Zelensky, 2022zz, 28:09–29:18). No European country, in his view, had a right to hold back from supporting Ukraine through all available means: "And the state that blocks this financing for Ukraine cannot have excuses. It should remember that it is a European state. And should fix this problem immediately" (Zelensky, 2022zza, 9:37–39:51). "Constant political pressure on Russia is needed," he argued, "to increase the number of countries participating in the anti-war coalition" (Zelensky, 2022zza, 7:28–37:35).

Because the conflict appeared in Zelensky's speeches as a war for "shared freedom . . . For Paris and Kyiv. For Berlin and Warsaw. For Madrid and Rome" (Zelensky, 2022l, 7:33–37:39), it was necessary "to act together, press together" (Zelensky, 2022l, 7:49–57:52). First, in his view, it was "necessary to arm those who are really fighting for freedom. For evil to lose" (Zelensky, 2022o, 11:47–11:53). With Ukraine presented as an integral part of the civilized world, not only the war itself but also the postwar reconstruction of Ukraine came to be seen as "not a local project, the project of one people, but a joint task of the entire world, of all countries that can say about themselves 'we are civilized'" (Zelensky, 2022zv, 8:33–38:50).

As is evident from the examples provided, Zelensky's discursive constructions set up Russia as a complete opposite of Ukraine, which he presented as an integral part of the global community of "civilized people"—the people of Zelensky's transnational populist project. The chain of equivalence characterizing Russia united such signifiers as barbaric, evil, savage, inhuman, tyrannical, unfree, aggressive, and non-modern. Regarding Ukraine, the chain of equivalence united signifiers like civilized, just, peaceful, free, future-oriented, decent, conscientious, and so forth. In other words, in Zelensky's discourse, Ukraine appeared as everything that Russia was not.

The discursive constructions of oppositional journalists and bloggers discussed in the next part of the book demonstrate the contingency of this presentation of the conflict. By establishing a solid, impermeable barrier between "barbaric Russia" and the "civilized world," with Russia seen as a radical outside of the global order, Zelensky's discourse created the conditions for "maximum separation" in which "no element in the system of equivalences enters into relations other than those of opposition to the elements of the other system" (Laclau & Mouffe, 1985, p. 129). Such discourse does not presuppose any negotiation; rather, it shuts down the common symbolical space necessary for dialogue. The final battle of good versus evil is not meant to be settled through diplomacy, after all, but by fighting to the bitter end.

One may argue, of course, that "maximum separation" occurred when Russia attacked Ukraine on February 24—not with Zelensky's belligerent rhetoric following horrific physical violence by Russian forces. However, as the next part of the book demonstrates, an alternative vision of the situation is also possible: Oppositional commentators trace the roots of the ongoing conflict to the Euromaidan, with its radical othering of Russia and Ukrainian Russophones. According to such an outlook, it is this destruction of the common symbolic space necessary for negotiation and compromise that brought first the Donbas war and then the full-fledged military conflict between Ukraine and Russia.

The biggest problem with the Armageddon story propagated by Zelensky with the help of global media is that it does not allow people around the world to make sense of the conflict: What is it all about? How did it start? What were the reasons for Russia to attack Ukraine, apart from some incomprehensible desire to conquer the whole world, including Europe, Asia, and America, as Zelensky suggests? Zelensky's representation of the conflict fails to provide any answers to such questions.

The War for Democracy: Tyranny Must Lose

Ukraine as a beacon of democracy was another nodal point that ensured the stability of Zelensky's war-related discourse. From the very beginning of SMO, Zelensky claimed that "the war in Ukraine is in general the war for . . . democracy and freedom" (Zelensky, 2022a, 0:17–18:25). "We are one of the largest countries in Europe. One of the most diverse. But united by democracy and respect for every person," argued Zelensky while appealing to the people of Spain (Zelensky, 2022r, 0:45–50:55). "Ukraine was and remains a pillar for democratic processes in our region. The two revolutions of 2004 [1] and 2014 stopped the spread of dictatorship in Ukraine," he claimed while speaking to the people of Portugal (Zelensky, 2022w, 9:39–49:54).

Ukraine "chose the path of democracy and European integration. We have not deviated from this path," Zelensky said in an address to the politicians and people of Albania (Zelensky, 2022z, 10:02–10:11). "We have an open democracy in our country"—such was his message for Nine Network on Australian TV (Zelensky, 2022y, 26:14–26;18). During a meeting with journalists on March 12, Zelensky boasted that Ukraine's democratic condition was "yet to be found" in many other democratic states, adding, "We have no control over the media" (Zelensky, 2022e, 46:35–46:46).

The goal of Russia, according to Zelensky, was to make sure that Ukraine "would never have democracy, that we would never have independence"—this is what he claimed while speaking to the politicians and people of Iceland (Zelensky, 2022zd, 4:43–44:50). In Zelensky's articulation, Russia's war against Ukraine was about "the destruction of Ukraine as a democracy," as he put it when speaking to French businessmen (Zelensky, 2022zzd, 6:42–46:53). "One can't kill people because they defend these values, democracy," he argued while addressing the participants of a strategic forum in Slovenia (Zelensky, 2022zzc, 19:49–19:58). "Now the fate of our country is being decided. The fate of our people. Will Ukrainians be free? Will they preserve their democracy?" he said to the US Congress (Zelensky, 2022h, 3:3–4:20).

"You see how Ukraine is fighting for democracy," he told the people of Switzerland (Zelensky, 2022i, 2:02–12:10). "We fight and we give our lives for the future of democracy and of the open world," repeated Zelensky in an interview for CBS (Zelensky, 2022zzf). "We are not just fighting for these values—freedom, democracy, human rights—we really believe in them," Zelensky told the members of the International Security Forum (Zelensky, 2022zi, 16:33–16:44). "These are not just mottos—they are engraved in our souls and hearts," he claimed (Zelensky, 2022zi, 16:45–16:54).

Addressing the politicians and people of Italy, Zelensky characterized the war in Ukraine as being about "the destruction of your values—not only ours. Democracy, human rights are the same values as ours" (Zelensky, 2022j, 5:30–35:39). "This is a war for freedom, for the principles of sovereignty, for the principles of international law, for democracy. I am sure that this is our common war with you," Zelensky claimed while speaking to the Yale CEO Summit (Zelensky, 2022zk, 2:26–32:33). In Zelensky's view, "the whole world fights for Ukraine because Ukraine is fighting for the whole world—for democracy, for freedom, and for life" (Zelensky, 2022zn, 4:57–65:05). "We are fighting for freedom not only for ourselves, but we are also fighting for the freedom of the entire democratic world," he said to the participants of the Cannes Film Festival (Zelensky, 2022zp, 1:23–31:30).

According to Zelensky, ensuring Ukraine's victory was "in the interest of all democracies, because democracies must be able to defend themselves." "Freedom must be armed," Zelensky maintained (Zelensky, 2022m, 5:12–15:14). "The democratic system may fail not only on our continent if there is no action," he argued (Zelensky, 2022zm, 9:00–9:06). "People feel . . . [that] . . . in the centuries-old confrontation between democracy and tyranny, something is happening that can become decisive," he asserted to the participants of the Athens Democracy Forum (Zelensky, 2022zzg, 1:07–11:19). "We will definitely win. . . . For the sake of a democratic free future," Zelensky assured Canadian students (Zelensky, 2022zr, 9:48–49:58). "We must never stop defending freedom and democracy," he proclaimed while speaking at the meeting of the European Council (Zelensky, 2022zzi, 9:50–59:55).

As with the nodal point "civilization" discussed earlier, Zelensky constructed Ukraine as a model of democratic governance, linking his country to such signifiers as freedom, respect, openness, human rights, dialogue, discussion, justice, life, and so forth. In contrast, Russia was connected to dictatorship, cruelty, tyranny, and subjugation—everything that Ukraine and the "civilized world" were not. By presenting Ukraine as a defender of European values, Zelensky not only portrayed Ukraine and Europe as inextricably tied together but also cast himself as a leader of this civilized community of people, whose interests his country's citizens were laying down their lives to defend. It is here that we observe the emergence of the transnational populist project dividing the globe into a sharp dichotomy of "good us"—those who share the values of freedom, democracy, and social justice—against an "evil them," who reject such values.

Leaving aside the fact that in Zelensky's "democratic Ukraine" oppositional media are equated to collaborators and shut down (see the following chapters), the problem with this strict dichotomization of the extremely complex global sociopolitical landscape is that it renders completely invisible all the nuances of the situation and the diversity of positions among those involved in it. With such dichotomization ascendant in mainstream discourse, it becomes all but impossible for global audiences to understand the conflict and contribute to effective solutions.

Uniting the World Around the Truth

An emphasis on the unity of the civilized and democratic world in its support for Ukraine amid the fight against tyranny and barbarism is the third nodal point sustaining Zelensky's populist discourse. "United Europe is definitely stronger than any tyranny," he claimed (Zelensky, 2022zq, 1:22–31:27). "Tyranny must lose. So that Europe could remain as it is. Free, united, and strong in diversity," Zelensky argued while addressing the politicians and people of Luxembourg (Zelensky, 2022zh, 12:27–12:44). "Perhaps for the first time in human history, we can now show the whole world and for a long time that democracies, united, can stop any tyranny," he maintained when receiving the Churchill Leadership Award (Zelensky, 2022zy, 16:14–16:25). "Europe cannot have Russian branches that split the EU from the inside," he declared, reproaching those among his European colleagues who resisted imposing sanctions on Russia and advising the EU on how to deal with such apostasy. "Europe should stop listening to any excuses from the officials of Budapest" (Zelensky, 2022n, 8:08–18:42), he insisted.

Similar to his presentation of "the whole civilized world" as an unproblematic totality holding an identical view of the conflict, Zelensky also constructed Ukraine in totalizing terms. On March 5, communicating with Western journalists, Zelensky asserted: "The fact is that this country is united. . . . Authorities are no more separated from the people. We are all one, we are all power of the people. We are all one country" (Zelensky, 2022c, 38:20–38:33). On March 22, during another meeting with foreign journalists, Zelensky argued that "We are all in the same emotion. We all know who a friend is. We all know who the enemy is" (Zelensky, 2022k, 17:22–17:33). "One thought, one friend, one enemy," Zelensky stated while speaking to Polish media. "This is an absolutely clear and transparent thing when you don't waste time on unnecessary dialogues. You know for sure: there is an enemy, there is a friend" (Zelensky, 2022x, 22:45–23:02).

These and numerous similar discursive constructions reveal Zelensky's antipathy toward "unnecessary dialogues" and "bureaucracy." Ukraine did "not have time [either] for bureaucratic procedures" (Zelensky, 2022zr, 17:49–17:54) or for "unnecessary dialogues" (Zelensky, 2022x, 22:57–22:59), he argued. However, he also acknowledged that both dialogue and bureaucracy are integral parts of the democratic process. "Democracy is dialogue. This is a discussion . . . [of] . . . different opinions. Democracy always breeds bureaucracy . . . because everything must be balanced," Zelensky asserted (Zelensky, 2022zzh, 24:12–24:34). In arguing that Ukraine did not have time for unnecessary dialogue or bureaucracy, Zelensky effectively acknowledged that Ukraine did not have time for democratic procedures. "To defend freedom and democracy in the state, sometimes it is necessary to act quickly and undemocratically," he argued (Zelensky, 2022zr, 31:17–31:30).

As the next part of the book shows, this line of reasoning is not merely academic—the prosecutions of dissenters have been carried out in the name of a "democracy" and "freedom" expected to come at some later time, after the war. However, Zelensky ruled out the possibility of democratic deliberation in the field of national security even after the conflict. "We must talk seriously about the rigid vertical of the security of our state. . . . There can be no liberal things here"—this is how he described his vision for the future of the Ukrainian state in a speech to Stanford University (Zelensky, 2022zg, 25:43–26:18), endorsing an anti-liberal and antidemocratic vertical of power in the sphere of national security even after the end of the war.

Speaking to the politicians and people of Indonesia, Zelensky argued that before the war Ukraine had been divided. "Western Ukraine, East, North, South. . . . But this war, this challenge—it united" the country, he said (Zelensky, 2022zf, 50:23–50:36). He made a similar claim during an interview with NBC: "After me, a united Ukraine, a united people will remain. Today, we do not divide people who are from the west of the country, who are from the center, who are from Donbas. We are all united" (Zelensky, 2022zu, 36:46–37:03). "We have become even more united now than ever, over the 31 years of our independence from the Soviet Union," Zelensky said in an interview for CBS (Zelensky, 2022zzf). "It is important that we have such an association in our society. It is very important that we are like-minded," he claimed while speaking to the *Economist* (Zelensky, 2022zw, 12:38–12:45). "Drivers, volunteers, stars, and journalists—they all became one profession. This profession is the Ukrainian," Zelensky told the participants of the annual meeting of the Yalta European Strategy Forum (Zelensky, 2022zze, 2:00–2:10).

On March 23, while speaking to the politicians and people of France, Zelensky announced that "We have no right and left today. We do not see who the government is and who is the opposition. Normal politics ended on the day of the Russian invasion and will only resume when there is peace" (Zelensky, 2022l, 8:03–8:18). Addressing the Parliament of Ukraine during Boris Johnson's visit to Kyiv, Zelensky proclaimed: "Today, we have one party. And this party is Ukraine. The one faction is Ukraine. The one mono-majority is Ukraine" (Zelensky, 2022za, 25:06–25:21). "I think that we will forget politics until peacetime, although it is better to forget forever," he maintained (Zelensky, 2022za, 24:02–24:12).

Such constructions demonstrate intolerance for political processes, which he constantly showed even before the war (Baysha, 2022). Through the utopia of absolute positivity, constructed discursively—a flawless society existing without pathology, complexity, or contradictions—Zelensky strove to create a perfectly sterile social universe not infected with politics and liberated from political antagonisms. In line with Mouffe's (2005) observation regarding "the post-political Zeitgeist" where "the political is played out in the moral register" (p. 4), the political contestation of alternative views has been substituted for the moralism of a belief in the perfect unity of Ukrainian society. The forces that ended up in opposition to his definition of the conflict have been attacked not politically (based on differing opinions) but morally (based on accusations of treasons). "In place of a struggle of 'right and left,' we are faced with a struggle between 'right and wrong'" (Mouffe, 2005, p. 4)—this has been the essence of "politics" within Zelensky's system of power even before February 24, 2022. After this day, the "post-political Zeitgeist" of Zelensky's authoritarian populism, which has now acquired a transnational dimension, only solidified and strengthened.

As soon as "authorities are no longer separated from the people" and "the government became the people," there is no longer any need for political representation or political struggles over meanings. Such contestations would be superfluous in Zelensky's imagined unified society where everything is perfected by the will of the enlightened ruler loved by his subjects: "We forgave each other a lot, we love each other," Zelensky said of his relationship with the people of Ukraine (Zelensky, 2022b, 0:45–50:51). Even before the ongoing war with Russia, Zelensky's government had little to do with political representation, as a result of which public opinion came to be completely ignored (Baysha, 2022); when this war started, the public itself was disregarded as the opinion of the people was equated to the ruler's: "The people became the government, the government became the people" (Zelensky, 2022k, 17:15–17:17). It is well-known that a government can only be challenged if it derives its sovereignty from representation. A lack of representation makes those in power unaccountable and cruel (Baudrillard, 2005)—something Ukrainian dissenters are well aware of, as the following chapters will show.

Talking about Ukraine's desire to join the EU, Zelensky also referred to the ostensible unity of Ukraine regarding this issue. "For me, the victory is Ukraine's accession to the EU. This is what the people of Ukraine want so much. They defended this right on the Maidan, during the revolutions," he said (Zelensky, 2022zc, 38:15–38:37). Later, while addressing Ukrainians on the occasion of the country being granted candidacy for EU membership, Zelensky explained that the European course for Ukraine was "the path fought for by the Revolution on Granite in the 1990s, [2] the Orange Revolution stood at the barricades in 2004, and the Heavenly Hundred [3] gave their lives during the Revolution of Dignity [Euromaidan] in 2014" (Zelensky, 2022zt, June 24, 10:56–11:11). "Ukraine decided to have a course to the EU by itself. And because of this—believe me—three revolutions took place. . . . People wanted to be in the EU. . . . It's their choice. The people's choice"—such was his message to the policy community of Indonesia (Zelensky, 2022zf, 53:55–54:26). Appealing to the participants of the EU Summit, Zelensky claimed:

> We Ukrainians believe in the EU, although we remained formally outside the EU, probably in our country there were the most flags of the united Europe. They were in the hands of our people during the revolutions, they were in our trenches since 2014.
>
> (Zelensky, 2022zs, 7:28–37:48)

"In 2014, the Ukrainian people defended and protected their European future," he said in his speech to Ukrainians upon EU candidacy (Zelensky, 2022zt, 8:30–38:37).

As explained in the first chapter, during the Euromaidan—or the Revolution of Dignity, as the pro-Maidan discourse dubbed it—Ukrainians were deeply divided in their attitudes toward the "European future" that has since been presented by Zelensky as the ardent desire of all the citizens of Ukraine. Although the onset of Russia's attack against Ukraine in February 2022 eroded the support for Russia among many hitherto pro-Russian Ukrainians (Tkachev, 2022), it is highly unlikely that the war with Russia would automatically unite all Ukrainians in a preference for European integration. The number of refugees moving to Russia—2.8 million people, the highest of any country receiving Ukrainians amid the conflict—suggests that this may not be the case (UNHCR, 2022). The number of Ukrainians accused of being "collaborators," whose arrests are regularly reported by both Ukraine and international organizations (Peters, 2022; UN, 2022), also testifies against this supposed unity. According to the Security Service of Ukraine (SSU), from February 24 to the middle of November, it started more than 18,000 criminal proceedings related to "crimes against national security," which include treason, sabotage, and assistance to the aggressor state (SSU, 2022). From time to time, reports about pro-Russian Ukrainians living in the southeastern regions appear even in mainstream media outlets of the West that otherwise support Zelensky's narrative regarding the conflict (e.g., Economist, 2023; Gibbons-Neff & Yermak, 2022; Miller & Schmidt, 2022).

Judging from Zelensky's communication with internal audiences (it is noteworthy that he has never discussed this with transnational publics), he is well aware that a hermetic unity of Ukraine exists only in his speeches and the discursive constructions of other propagandists. Here are some examples that illustrate this point:

> On April 5, while communicating with Ukrainian journalists, Zelensky acknowledged: "If you take the people who are fighting with us, some people—unfortunately—who have become separatists, they are more wicked than the Russian military."
>
> (Zelensky, 2022s, 34:06–35:20)

> On April 16, during another meeting with Ukrainian journalists, Zelensky confessed that he had "many questions about Donbas. What do we want from this and what do our people want? There are people who hate us there."
>
> (Zelensky, 2022v, 25:15–25:25)

> On June 6, at a similar meeting, Zelensky stated: "Among Russian-speaking people in the east of our country—even where there are attacks, even now—there is a percentage of those who still doubt what is happening. . . . After we banned several Russian channels through sanctions . . . this audience will continue to look for Russian-language information. It is very important that this [information] space be occupied by *true channels*."
>
> (Zelensky, 2022zj, 9:45–10:41, emphasis added)

Zelensky does not explain why many people of Donbas "hate" Ukraine, why Donbas fighters are "more wicked than the Russian military," or why many Russian speakers in the east of Ukraine doubt the explanation of the war provided by Ukraine's official channels of information. Answering these questions would ruin the coherence of his one-dimensional Manichean construction of the conflict, according to which it is a war between civilization and barbarism, democracy and tyranny, and good and evil. This is what "true channels," both local and global, have been relentlessly repeating after Zelensky.

The importance of focusing on and disseminating the "truth" was highlighted by Zelensky every time he spoke to journalists, both Ukrainian and foreign. "The truth is on our side" (Zelensky, 2022e, 46:04–46:05) has been one of Zelensky's central messages for the world. "Friends of Ukraine, friends of truth"—this is how he addressed the parliament of Canada (Zelensky,

2022g, 9:32–39:37). "Our strength is in the truth," he told the participants of the Joint Expeditionary Force meeting (March15a, 13:38–13:40). "You will be on the side of peace, truth, which means goodness," Zelensky promised Danish journalists, asking them to support Ukraine (Zelensky, 2022zo, 3:06–33:09). "We want the countries of the African continent to support not just Ukraine, but to support the truth"—such was his message to African journalists (Zelensky, 2022zz, 12:05–12:11). "To unite the world around the truth" was, in Zelensky's view, the mission of Ukraine (Zelensky, 2022zc, 56:29–56:33).

As the next part of the book illustrates, Zelensky's representation of the conflict is not objective truth but a discursive construction that can be contested. It shows that the mythology of the final fight between the united forces of civilization and democracy against tyranny and barbarism, as propagated by Zelensky, is only one possible definition of the ongoing war; the possibility of alternative articulations also exists. The condition of possibility for Zelensky's discourse to be accepted as a normal judgment by millions of people within his transnational community of "civilized people" has been the exclusion of alternative meanings and the "others" who express them.

To put it in Laclau and Mouffe's terms, the repression of oppositional journalists in post-Maidan Ukraine (discussed in the following chapters) is a continuing attempt to arrest the flow of difference, to close the discourse, and to establish stable meanings favorable to Ukraine's official political course. However, as the cases discussed in the following chapters suggest, it is impossible, within the digital environment of interconnected information networks, to close discourse fully and establish meanings that remain forever fixed.

This impossibility manifests itself in the revival of oppositional discourse in new discursive-material configurations that cannot be controlled by the government. Oppositional journalists and bloggers who were able to flee Ukraine now run their media channels from abroad; all of those who are still able to work moved to Telegram—a platform beyond the reach of the Ukrainian government. It is noteworthy that the popularity of Telegram among Ukrainians has grown significantly since the beginning of the ongoing war (Krat, 2022), which, as engaged observers argue, may reflect people's dissatisfaction with the one-dimensionality of Ukraine's official propaganda (Resident, 2022). With the adoption in December 2022 of the new media law of Ukraine, which contradicts the Constitution and establishes censorship in the information space (Guz, 2022), Telegram's popularity in Ukraine is set to increase further as it will be the only channel offering an alternative to the official perspective while opposition channels on other platforms, such as YouTube and Facebook, have been increasingly blocked in Ukraine. The next part of the book will discuss these developments in greater detail.

Notes

1 The Orange Revolution of 2004 began on the eve of the second round of the presidential election, when the official count differed substantially from the results of exit polling that gave oppositional candidate Victor Yushchenko a lead of up to 11 percentage points. The official results gave the election win to Victor Yanukovych—the protégé of then incumbent President Leonid Kuchma—by 3 points. Huge protests against what was seen by the protesters as "massive fraud" resulted in Yushchenko's victory.
2 The Revolution on Granite (or Student Revolution on Granite) involved a hunger strike and mass protests of the Ukrainian Soviet youth in 1990. Among the protesters' main demands were the nationalization of the property of the Communist Party of Ukraine and the holding of new elections for the Supreme Soviet of the Ukrainian SSR based on a multiparty system.
3 "Heaven's Hundred" refers to the revolutionaries killed on the Maidan in February 2014.

Reference List

Baudrillard, J. (2005). *The intelligence of evil*. Berg.
Baysha, O. (2022). *Democracy, populism, and neoliberalism in Ukraine: On the fringes of the virtual and the real*. Routledge.
Economist. (2023, January 19). *Uncertain allegiance: Some liberated Ukrainian regions have mixed loyalties*. www.economist.com/europe/2023/01/19/some-liberated-ukrainian-regions-have-mixed-loyalties
Gibbons-Neff, T., & Yermak, N. (2022, December 8). A gray area of loyalties splinters a liberated Ukrainian town. *New York Times*. www.nytimes.com/2022/12/08/world/europe/ukraine-russia-loyalty-sviatohirsk.html
Guz, S. (2022, November 7). Ukraine's proposed new media law threatens press freedom. *Open Democracy*. www.opendemocracy.net/en/odr/ukraine-media-law-press-freedom/
Krat, V. (2022, November 17). Millions of Ukrainians still read enemy Telegram channels (in Ukrainian). *Ukrainian National News*. www.unn.com.ua/uk/news/2003478-milyoni-ukrayintsiv-dosi-chitayut-vorozhi-tel egram-kanali-minoboroni
Laclau, E., & Mouffe, C. (2001/1985). *Hegemony and socialist strategy: Towards a radical democratic politics*. Verso.
Miller, M., & Schmidt, S. (2022, November 22). In Kherson city, sympathies for Russia complicate reintegration into Ukraine. *Washington Post*. www.washingtonpost.com/world/2022/11/22/kherson-city-sympathies-russia-complicate-reintegration-into-ukraine/
Mouffe, C. (2005). *On the political*. Routledge.
Peters, A. (2022, November 10). Ukraine hunts for "collaborators." *World Socialist Web Site*. www.wsws.org/en/articles/2022/11/10/xpmh-n10.html
Resident. (2022, November 20). The technologists of the office of the President have a big problem (in Russian}. *Telegram*. https://t.me/rezident_ua/15208
SSU. (2022). SSU's results since the start of Russia's full-scale invasion. *Security Service of Ukraine*. https://ssu.gov.ua/en
Tkachev, Y. (2022, February 25). Apart from the military situation . . . (in Russian). *Telegram*. https://t.me/dadzibao/5624

UN. (2022, July 5). Ukraine: High commissioner updates human rights council. *United Nations Human Rights Office of the High Commissioner.* www.ohchr.org/en/statements/2022/07/ukraine-high-commissioner-updates-human-rights-council

UNHCR. (2022, November 22). Ukraine refugee situation. *The UN Refugee Agency.* https://data.unhcr.org/en/situations/ukraine

Zelensky, V. (2022a, March 1). Frank interview of Zelensky for CNN and Reuters (in Ukrainian). *YouTube.* www.youtube.com/watch?v=cAoplPOZrdo

Zelensky, V. (2022b, March 2). Today, Ukrainians are a symbol of resilience (in Ukrainian). *YouTube.* www.youtube.com/watch?v=I7G2lfWfkl4

Zelensky, V. (2022c, March 5). Volodymyr Zelenskyy spoke with representatives of the Western media (in Ukrainian). *YouTube.* www.youtube.com/watch?v=Z-R4sh2z0EM

Zelensky, V. (2022d, March 11). Volodymyr Zelensky's address to the Polish Sejm (in Ukrainian). *YouTube.* www.youtube.com/watch?v=qyfOUVmX3Kw

Zelensky, V. (2022e, March 12). Volodymyr Zelensky's conversation with journalists in the President's Office (in Ukrainian). *YouTube.* www.youtube.com/watch?v=rlSv0ImkfuI

Zelensky, V. (2022f, March 15a). Volodymyr Zelenskyy speaks at the meeting of the leaders of the joint expeditionary force (in Ukrainian). *YouTube.* www.youtube.com/watch?v=pWXFg4K1U6Q

Zelensky, V. (2022g, March 15b). Zelensky appealed to the Canadian government and Parliament (in Ukrainian). *YouTube.* www.youtube.com/watch?v=TSS6UV_mZzA&t=2s

Zelensky, V. (2022h, March 16). Volodymyr Zelensky spoke before the US Congress (in Ukrainian). *YouTube.* www.youtube.com/watch?v=HILlSCcphUc

Zelensky, V. (2022i, March 19). Volodymyr Zelensky turned to the people of Switzerland (in Ukrainian). *YouTube.* www.youtube.com/watch?v=_hmIELNafLQ

Zelensky, V. (2022j, March 22a). Volodymyr Zelensky's address to the people and politicians of Italy (in Ukrainian). *YouTube.* www.youtube.com/watch?v=Anmx0rvpFZA

Zelensky, V. (2022k, March 22b). Volodymyr Zelensky's interview to global public media (in Ukrainian). *YouTube.* www.youtube.com/watch?v=ODC2-KpmxvE&t=2s

Zelensky, V. (2022l, March 23). Volodymyr Zelensky addressed the people and politicians of France (in Ukrainian). *YouTube.* www.youtube.com/watch?v=6M8hURo52Hc

Zelensky, V. (2022m, March 24). Volodymyr Zelensky's address to G-7 (in Ukrainian). *YouTube.* www.youtube.com/watch?v=69yIZUczAcU

Zelensky, V. (2022n, March 29). Volodymyr Zelensky addressed politicians and the people of Denmark (in Ukrainian). *YouTube.* www.youtube.com/watch?v=8RNE5t0NG6M

Zelensky, V. (2022o, March 31a). Volodymyr Zelensky addressed the people and politicians of Australia (in Ukrainian). *YouTube.* www.youtube.com/watch?v=omhUiWOC_-M

Zelensky, V. (2022p, March 31b). Volodymyr Zelensky addressed the people and politicians of Belgium (in Ukrainian). *YouTube.* www.youtube.com/watch?v=QBA6KlrsBDw

Zelensky, V. (2022q, March 31c). Volodymyr Zelensky addressed the people and politicians of the Netherlands (in Ukrainian). *YouTube.* www.youtube.com/watch?v=BOMy1vUAQdA

Zelensky, V. (2022r, April 5a). President of Ukraine Volodymyr Zelensky addressed the people and politicians of Spain (in Ukrainian). *YouTube.* www.youtube.com/watch?v=AXPdGxwtIsU

Zelensky, V. (2022s, April 5b). President Volodymyr Zelensky spoke with representatives of Ukrainian media (in Ukrainian). *YouTube*. www.youtube.com/watch?v=xIw0vJScEJo

Zelensky, V. (2022t, April 8). Volodymyr Zelensky addressed the people and politicians of Finland (in Ukrainian). *YouTube*. www.youtube.com/watch?v=Tgkwlk68igg

Zelensky, V. (2022u, April 11). Volodymyr Zelensky addressed the people and politicians of the Republic of Korea (in Ukrainian). *YouTube*. www.youtube.com/watch?v=Sc2Qlglajc8

Zelensky, V. (2022v, April 16). President Volodymyr Zelensky talked with Ukrainian journalists (in Ukrainian). *YouTube*. www.youtube.com/watch?v=PW1MESME4aU&t=2s

Zelensky, V. (2022w, April 21). To the Portuguese. Address of the President of Ukraine Volodymyr Zelensky (in Ukrainian). *YouTube*. www.youtube.com/watch?v=fjfe7XnglkE

Zelensky, V. (2022x, April 29). Volodymyr Zelensky spoke with representatives of the Polish mass media (in Ukrainian). *YouTube*. www.youtube.com/watch?v=uobFhTgr96k

Zelensky, V. (2022y, May 2). Volodymyr Zelensky's interview for the 60 minutes project of the Australian television channel nine network (in Ukrainian). *YouTube*. www.youtube.com/watch?v=iRtp89_ZspA

Zelensky, V. (2022z, May 3a). Volodymyr Zelensky addressed the people and politicians of Albania (in Ukrainian). *YouTube*. www.youtube.com/watch?v=s1bIIb1AlEA

Zelensky, V. (2022za, May 3b). Volodymyr Zelensky thanked Boris Johnson and Great Britain for their support and assistance to Ukraine (in Ukrainian). *YouTube*. www.youtube.com/watch?v=-ndjVtbJi74

Zelensky, V. (2022zb, May 4). Speech by the President of Ukraine Volodymyr Zelensky at the *Wall Street Journal* CEO council summit session (in Ukrainian). *YouTube*. www.youtube.com/watch?v=SXskLGTvbPE

Zelensky, V. (2022zc, May 6a). The president took part in the conference of analytical centers of Great Britain at Chatham House (in Ukrainian). *YouTube*. www.youtube.com/watch?v=XrQzIm1O0UU

Zelensky, V. (2022zd, May 6b). President of Ukraine Volodymyr Zelensky addressed the people and politicians of Iceland (in Ukrainian). *YouTube*. www.youtube.com/watch?v=ZH4FjlvCSmU

Zelensky, V. (2022ze, May 22). To Ukrainians and Poles. Volodymyr Zelensky's speech in the Verkhovna Rada (in Ukrainian). *YouTube*. www.youtube.com/watch?v=GRpI9P1GqGU

Zelensky, V. (2022zf, May 27a). The president spoke at the foreign policy community of Indonesia analytical center (in Ukrainian). *YouTube*. www.youtube.com/watch?v=N_Ckjx8h1KU

Zelensky, V. (2022zg, May 27b). To the Stanford research community and students. Address of Volodymyr Zelensky (in Ukrainian). *YouTube*. www.youtube.com/watch?v=YEvACdjK9YA

Zelensky, V. (2022zh, June 2a). President of Ukraine Volodymyr Zelensky addressed the politicians and people of Luxembourg (in Ukrainian). *YouTube*. www.youtube.com/watch?v=4sa0Dwx2Db4

Zelensky, V. (2022zi, June 2b). To the international security forum. Speech of Volodymyr Zelensky (in Ukrainian). *YouTube*. www.youtube.com/watch?v=uNdsXHfEeNQ

Zelensky, V. (2022zj, June 6). Volodymyr Zelensky's conversation with media representatives on journalist's day (in Ukrainian). *YouTube*. www.youtube.com/watch?v=yrNA01enl04

Zelensky, V. (2022zk, June 8). Volodymyr Zelensky took part in the Yale CEO Summit (in Ukrainian). *YouTube*. www.youtube.com/watch?v=6fdRHLeas8s

Zelensky, V. (2022zl, June 10a). Communication of Volodymyr Zelensky with students and professors of educational institutions of Great Britain (in Ukrainian). *YouTube*. www.youtube.com/watch?v=pyRXw_cxhxU

Zelensky, V. (2022zm, June 10b). Zelensky addressed the participants of the Copenhagen democratic summit (in Ukrainian). *YouTube*. www.youtube.com/watch?v=Z7a4l7KpATU

Zelensky, V. (2022zn, June 12). To the CORE organization. Address of Volodymyr Zelensky (in Ukrainian). *YouTube*. www.youtube.com/watch?v=AS99ie5XnCk

Zelensky, V. (2022zo, June 14). Zelensky gave an online press conference for Danish media (in Ukrainian). *YouTube*. www.youtube.com/watch?v=7e0X_FQPpXo

Zelensky, V. (2022zp, June 21). Zelensky's address to the participants of the Cannes Lions International Festival of Creativity (in Ukrainian). *YouTube*. www.youtube.com/watch?v=ATQ95CCuGR4

Zelensky, V. (2022zq, June 22a). Zelensky addressed the participants of the Embrace Ukraine charity telethon (in Ukrainian). *YouTube*. www.youtube.com/watch?v=_i3zJz6nmkM

Zelensky, V. (2022zr, June 22b). Zelensky talked with the student community of leading universities in Canada (in Ukrainian). *YouTube*. www.youtube.com/watch?v=jHNnMoKZLXI

Zelensky, V. (2022zs, June 23). Zelensky addressed the participants of the EU summit after granting Ukraine the status of a candidate for membership (in Ukrainian). *YouTube*. www.youtube.com/watch?v=00RneYV7Szc

Zelensky, V. (2022zt, June 24). Ukraine is a candidate for joining the European Union! (in Ukrainian). *YouTube*. www.youtube.com/watch?v=RoJO_UfD4u8&t=1s

Zelensky, V. (2022zu, June 29). Zelensky's interview for the American TV channel NBC (in English). *YouTube*. www.youtube.com/watch?v=lWzbPR5Hxoc

Zelensky, V. (2022zv, July 4). Zelensky speaking at the conference on food innovation of Ukraine in Lugano (in Ukrainian). *YouTube*. www.youtube.com/watch?v=LLoOFKBQPjY

Zelensky, V. (2022zw, July 5). Zelensky took part in the economist's 26th annual government roundtable (in Ukrainian). *YouTube*. www.youtube.com/watch?v=jUwhdxmkb3U

Zelensky, V. (2022zx, July 8). Volodymyr Zelensky's interview for CNN (in Ukrainian). *YouTube*. www.youtube.com/watch?v=APhoEEH3gGE

Zelensky, V. (2022zy, July 26). Zelensky's speech at the ceremony of the Churchill Award for Leadership (in Ukrainian). *YouTube*. www.youtube.com/watch?v=m7YiGDS_how

Zelensky, V. (2022zz, August 4). Zelensky spoke with media representatives from Nigeria, South Africa, Kenya and Ghana (in Ukrainian). *YouTube*. www.youtube.com/watch?v=XmDAunwxtec

Zelensky, V. (2022zza, August 11). Zelensky spoke at the donor conference of Ukraine's allies from Northern Europe (in Ukrainian). *YouTube*. www.youtube.com/watch?v=_5fOqAvVdxk

Zelensky, V. (2022zzb, August 24). Zelensky spoke at a meeting of the UN Security Council (in Ukrainian). *YouTube*. www.youtube.com/watch?v=6tPIH1OOZGs

Zelensky, V. (2022zzc, August 29a). Zelensky addressed the participants of the strategic forum in bled, Slovenia (in Ukrainian). *YouTube*. www.youtube.com/watch?v=a23K-WJg6Go

Zelensky, V. (2022zzd, August 29b). Volodymyr Zelensky's address to the "movement of enterprises of France" (in Ukrainian). *YouTube*. www.youtube.com/watch?v=tpFcioLNFes

Zelensky, V. (2022zze, September 10). Volodymyr Zelensky spoke at the annual meeting of the Yalta European Strategy (in Ukrainian). *YouTube*. www.youtube.com/watch?v=8keVB7vz7Ys

Zelensky, V. (2022zzf, September 25). The full transcript of an interview with Ukrainian President Volodymyr Zelensky…on "Face the Nation." *CBS*. www.cbsnews.com/news/volodymyr-zelenskyy-ukraine-president-face-the-nation-transcript-09-25-2022/

Zelensky, V. (2022zzg, September 28). Zelensky addressed the participants of the Athens democratic forum (in Ukrainian). *YouTube*. www.youtube.com/watch?v=gW-Z0JeENwM

Zelensky, V. (2022zzh, October 6). To the Lowy institute. Volodymyr Zelensky's address (in Ukrainian). *YouTube*. www.youtube.com/watch?v=NwhWZPXnNDw

Zelensky, V. (2022zzi, October 7). Zelensky spoke during the meeting of the European council (in Ukrainian). *YouTube*. www.youtube.com/watch?v=w98ZmpOCbvs&t=2s

Zelensky, V. (2022zzj, October 14). Zelensky gave an interview for the German public television ZDF (in Ukrainian). *YouTube*. www.youtube.com/watch?app=desktop&v=ChravochNnE

Part II

Alternative Articulations of the Russia–Ukraine Conflict

4 Ukraine Under External Control

A "Revolution of Dignity" Indistinguishable From a "Coup D'état"

As is evident from the previous chapter, one of the dominant frames of reference for the ongoing war between Russia and Ukraine, as employed by Zelensky in his attempt to create a global anti-Russia coalition, was the presentation of this war as a fight between tyranny and democracy in which the (Euro)Maidan revolution of 2014 served as an important point of reference. In Zelensky's discursive constructions, the Maidan has been connected to the idea of popular struggle for democracy and freedom, with the people acting on their desire to liberate themselves from tyranny, establish social justice, and so on. What Zelensky completely ignored in his valorization of the Maidan as a symbol of Ukraine's collective will for a better life is that oppositional views of this development also exist, although in contemporary Ukraine they are not only silenced but also criminalized. Since the victory of the revolution, oppositional journalists and bloggers have been intimidated, prosecuted, and jailed. Many of them were forced to flee Ukraine. This chapter will consider several discursive constructions by such oppositional figures.

Oles Buzina

The first name that comes to mind in connection with the annihilation of "otherness" in post-Maidan Ukraine is Oles Buzina—a famous Ukrainian writer, publicist, and journalist who was killed by radicals on April 16, 2015, near his apartment building in the center of Kyiv (Reuters, 2015). Shortly before the murder, his private address had been made public by the nationalistic website *Myrotvorets*, which was launched "by a people's deputy holding a position of adviser to the Ministry of Interior of Ukraine," according to a UN report (UN OHCHR, 2018, p. 15). *Myrotvorets* has been part of the general strategy of intimidating opponents of the Maidan. Anybody deemed an "enemy of the people"—anybody who dares to express anti-Maidan views publicly or

DOI: 10.4324/9781003379164-7

challenge Ukraine's nationalistic agenda—may appear on this website. The site was not shut down even after an international scandal when *Myrotvorets* published the personal data of well-known foreign politicians such as former Chancellor of Germany Gerhard Schröder (Deutsche Welle, 2018).

Buzina's killers were found and arrested in 2015; but later, at the request of "activists," they were released. This is how one of the reports on the human rights in Ukraine by the US State Department describes the situation: "Authorities detained but later released two suspects in the 2015 killing in Kyiv of Oles Buzina, who was perceived as pro-Russian. Both suspects were allegedly members of right-wing political groups" (DOS, 2016). The thing is that in post-Maidan Ukraine, right-wing "activists" who go after "enemies of the people" are considered heroes, and their illegal actions are very rarely punished.

From the point of view of these "activists," Buzina was obviously an "enemy of the people"—the term had already been equated exclusively with the foes of the Maidan and supporters of Russia. In his blog posts and public speeches, Buzina advocated for a closer political association between Ukraine and Russia, ridiculed the primitiveness of nationalist ideology, and campaigned for legislation prohibiting neo-Nazi organizations (Buzina, 2009). He identified himself as both a Ukrainian and a Russian—before the Maidan, such a double identification was normal for millions of Ukrainians, which is explained by the deep historical connections between the two states (Plokhy, 2008). In fact, Zelensky himself argued in 2014 that "Ukrainians and Russians are the same people" (Sharij, 2021a, 8:27–28:30).

For the aim of my analysis in this book—to activate the silenced meanings that could destabilize Zelensky's populist discourse and provide alternative insights for understanding the ongoing conflict—I selected one of the most interesting television programs featuring Buzina, in which he clashed with the famous Russian nationalist Vladimir Zhirinovsky. The "Duel" (this was the name of the program) was aired by one of the main Russian TV channels, Russia-1, on January 30, 2014—three weeks before the victory of the Euromaidan.

The main thesis pushed forward by Buzina in the show was that the Maidan had been staged by the United States, and that Russia must help Ukraine to defend its sovereignty. "Do you know what we are suffocating without in Ukraine now?" he asked the audience. "Without the support of Russia. . . . No, there is no need to send tanks, no parachute divisions. . . . We can handle this. Stop America. At the diplomatic level" (Buzina, 2014, 15:15–15:33). Zhirinovsky responded that the situation was none of Russia's business, that Ukraine was free to join Europe if it wanted and that NATO rather than Russia could provide support in the future. Zhirinovsky's followers backed up their leader by arguing that if Ukraine wanted to be with Russia, it should make its own effort to stand up to the West, not wait passively for help from Moscow.

Astonished by Zhirinovsky and his fellow party members drawing a solid dividing line between Russians and Ukrainians, Buzina invoked a famous quote from the 19th-century Russian-Ukrainian writer Nikolai Gogol: "I don't know which soul is bigger in me, the hohol's [¹] or the Russian's." "Should I divide myself from inside?" Buzina went on. "There are two states, but there is one people. And there are the intrigues of the West," he claimed (Buzina, 2014, 55:07–55:35).

Dismissing the charges of cowardice directed at pro-Russian Ukrainians who seemed not to be fighting against the Maidan revolution although they viewed it as a coup d'état, Buzina (2014) informed the audience that self-defense units were being formed in Ukraine, claiming that two-thirds of Ukrainians were for Russia (Buzina, 2014, 39:25–40:00). When the show's host, Vladimir Solovyov—one of the main Russian propagandists—asked for the names of Ukrainians who had refused to kneel before the country's radicals, Buzina rebuffed him by saying it was extremely dangerous at the time to reveal these names. According to him, radicals were posting online the names of all the Berkut soldiers² and internal troops stationed on the Maidan. "They call for killing their wives, kill their children, beat them," Buzina asserted (2014, 1:16:16–17:16:59). Buzina also told the audience that, while visiting Moscow, he had been getting warning messages about radicals waiting for him at the station in the city of Kyiv. "My life is in mortal danger," Buzina asserted. "And I don't know if I will be alive tomorrow or not" (Buzina, 2014, 54:19–54:50).

He would be killed a little more than a year after pronouncing these ominous words. He witnessed the beginning of Ukraine's "anti-terrorist operation" against Donbas and lamented the development, as did millions of other Ukrainians, especially in the eastern regions. Not long before his death, Buzina (2015) wrote the poem "I don't like this version of Ukraine." Here are some excerpts:

I don't like the soot of the Maidan,
I don't like its bloody chaos.
This wound is gaping for a year now
It's bleeding thousands of lives. . . .

I don't like these Kiev tanks
That iron my Donbass and shell its cities. . . .

I don't like this version of Ukraine
Where fascism has not been beaten . . .

I don't like the strategists from the Pentagon
Enjoying profits from the "war on terror . . ."

I don't like the Yankees in Ukraine
They lynch it in their usual manner.

Unlike Zelensky, who linked the Maidan to the ideas of democracy, liberty, human dignity, and the like, Buzina connected it to entirely different associations: the West's intrusion into Ukraine's sovereign affairs, ultra-nationalism/radicalism/extremism/fascism whose funding was drawn from U.S. coffers, the persecution of dissent, chaos, death, and, finally, Ukraine's war against Donbas and the suffering of its people.

Oles Buzina has been dead for more than seven years now, but the anti-Maidan discourse he propagated is not. As I show in the following sections of this book, the links between the Maidan and such signifiers as coup d'état, external control, radicalism, Ukraine's war against Donbas, and so forth—everything that Zelensky, along with other post-Maidan leaders and global media, has been trying to bury under the mythology of a "people's democratic uprising"[3]—are being articulated in the discourse of those anti-Maidan "others" who, unlike Buzina, are still able to speak.

But before I move to their discursive constructions, I would like to highlight one aspect that is crucially important for understanding the complexity of the Ukrainian situation with respect to anti-Maidan "others." Their status as "enemies of the people" in post-Maidan Ukraine does not necessarily mean they have been applauded in Russia. It is noteworthy that, in a studio of a mainstream television channel of Russia, Buzina was attacked by one of the most popular Russian public figures, Vladimir Zhirinovsky, who—like Ukrainian nationalists—also drew a solid dividing line between Ukrainians and Russians. This illustrates the invalidity of Ukraine's official narrative that presents all pro-Russian and anti-Maidan Ukrainians as dancing to the tune of Russian propaganda. Numerous similar stories, some of which will be considered later, reveal the same pattern—after becoming pariahs in post-Maidan Ukraine, Ukrainians with anti-Maidan views have not necessarily been seen as friends by those who hold power and influence in Russia. The reality on the ground has always been much more complicated than depicted by either Ukrainian or Russian propagandists.

The War in Donbas: A War on Terror or a Civil War?

One fixture in Zelensky's speeches to international audiences has been highlighting the claim that Russia started the war against Ukraine in 2014, which is in line with the dominant narrative of the post-Maidan Ukrainian government. According to Zelensky, the war has been going on since 2014, when Russia "seized our Crimean Peninsula and started a war in Donbas" (Zelensky, 2022b, 9:40–59:47). Zelensky has never mentioned that the uprising in Donbas began as a local reaction by the people of Donbas to the Euromaidan's overturning of the government in Kyiv, and that Ukraine itself started the war in the region by launching its "anti-terrorist operation." The discourse of Russia's "brutal and unprovoked aggression" (Zelensky, 2022a, 1:40–41:57) against democratic, civilized, and freedom-loving Ukraine has sedimented within the post-Maidan public sphere of Ukraine to the point of becoming the normal judgment. To question publicly this normalized mythology today means to put oneself in the position of a "collaborator" and "traitor." However, alternative articulations still exist in the oppositional discourse of anti-Maidan "others," although those who propagate it are now physically outside of Ukraine. Video blogs by Ruslan Kotsaba, a former political prisoner now in the USA, are useful in excavating the meanings excluded from Zelensky's discursive constructions.

Ruslan Kotsaba

Ruslan Kotsaba is a Ukrainian journalist from Ivano-Frankivsk, a city in Western Ukraine whose residents overwhelmingly supported the Euromaidan revolution. Originally, Kotsaba was also its proponent; he was on the Maidan from the first days of the protests, although—as he acknowledged later—like most other protesters, he had not read the Association Agreement over which the revolution was initiated (Montyan, 2020, 29:41–30:15). The transformation of his views began there, on-site, when he started questioning the legality and validity of the violent actions of protesters, including their setting policemen on fire with Molotov cocktails (Montyan, 2020, 33:15–33:30).

In the summer of 2014, Kotsaba visited Donbas. His communications with local people convinced him that the conflict was a civil war—not an "anti-terrorist operation" and not a war between Russia and Ukraine, as Ukrainian propaganda maintained (Kotsaba, 2014). In 2015, he posted on YouTube a video calling for a mass boycott against military mobilization. He was arrested and held on suspicion of undermining national security. In May 2016, Kotsaba was sentenced to three and a half years in prison with confiscation of his property. After 524 days in captivity, he was acquitted in the Court of Appeal and released in July 2016 (Chambers & Freedom, 2022). Despite Amnesty International (2015) recognizing Kotsaba as a prisoner of conscience, the case was reopened by a superior court of Ukraine in 2017 and the trial recommenced in 2021. Shortly before the beginning of the war with Russia in February 2022, the state prosecution was suspended, though not entirely concluded. On several occasions, Kotsaba has been attacked and beaten by radicals/"activists" who accuse him of treason and collaborating with Russia (Council of Europe, 2021). As an "enemy of the people," Kotsaba was put on *Myrotvorets* in March 2016 (Kotsaba, 2016).

For the purposes of my analysis, I have chosen two of Kotsaba's videos. The first, from 2015, is the one in which he calls on Ukrainians to resist military mobilization; the other one is from 2022, recorded just days before the start of the ongoing war. In his 2015 video, Kotsaba said it would be easier for him to serve two to five years in prison than go to the civil war and kill or assist in the killing of his countrymen who live in the east—even if they thought differently, even if they thought the Kyiv authorities were unworthy, and even if they had decided not to obey. "Let the SSU tell me that I am a spy, that I am an accomplice of Putin, that I am playing into Putin's hands, I will still say this to everyone who hears me. I refuse to mobilize," Kotsaba proclaimed. It was impossible, Kotsaba argued, that in the 21st century, people would kill other people just because they wanted to live separately (Kotsaba, 2015, 4:22–24:31).

Kotsaba declared on camera what in 2015 already carried substantial risk of consequences to say in Ukraine—calling the war in Donbas a "civil war" was by that time perceived as Russian propaganda and equated to treason. This is why journalistic trips to Donbas were not encouraged, to put it mildly; as soon as Donbas rebels were labeled "terrorists," any communication with them came to be seen as "complicity in terrorism." Only the very few journalists who had the fortitude not to be intimidated by Ukrainian authorities visited Donbas to see the situation with their own eyes. This, however, came at the expense of legal prosecutions, prison terms, and expulsion from Ukraine by the post-Maidan government.

On February 18, 2022, just six days before the current war started, Kotsaba uploaded to YouTube a video addressing Zelensky. He explained his decision to do so by saying he considered Zelensky a pacifist—a person who "four times in a row . . . ignored the mobilization summons that came during 2014 and 2015, when ordinary working people were used as cannon fodder," as Kotsaba (2022, 1:17–18:32) put it. Indeed, in its public statement during the 2019 presidential election, Ukraine's Ministry of Defense informed Ukrainians that four draft notices had been sent to Zelensky and that he "did not come to the military commissariat on his summons" (Radio Liberty, 2019). A video in which the future president is laughing at his draft summons during his comedy show is still available on the Internet (Aleks Orange, 2019).

"I want to remind you," Kotsaba went on, "There are crimes without a statute of limitations. . . . When the country's own army is used against its civilian population. In our country, the military forces of Ukraine are used against the civilian population" (Kotsaba, 2022, 1:50–52:02). Invoking Zelensky's promise during his presidential campaign to bring Ukrainians peace, Kotsaba argued: "As a president of peace, you have a chance . . . to spit on everything and say, 'You know what? I promised you that if I would not succeed and there is no peace, I will resign.'," he said (Kotsaba, 2022, 5:54–56:07). "War is a crime against humanity. War is a crime against Ukraine. And the one who accepts war is either a clinical moron . . . or a person who makes money from war," Kotsaba maintained, asking Zelensky to end the Donbas war through negotiations. "If it doesn't work out for you with some advisers, with these negotiations, change the clowns. [4] Take people not from *95th Quarter* [5]" he suggested (Kotsaba, 2022, 6:50–67:17).

As is evident from these examples, Kotsaba articulated the Maidan by linking it to illegality, injustice, persecution of dissent, the Donbas war, and people's suffering. The difference between the discursive constructions by Buzina and Kotsaba is that the former highlighted the link between the Maidan and external control over Ukraine, while Kotsaba focused on the amorality of the Ukrainian government: its double standards and lies. In Kotsaba's presentation, the ongoing war in Donbas was strongly linked to Zelensky's cynicism (ignoring his own summons with impunity but having no qualms about conscripting other people), lies (abandoning his pre-election promises), amorality (leading the country into a war rather than acknowledging his inability to secure peace and resigning as promised), and lack of professionalism (engaging in political theater instead of meaningful negotiations).

Ruslan Kotsaba has never supported Russia's SMO; however, he considers it a logical consequence of Ukraine's unwillingness to stop the war in Donbas through negotiation and compromise (more on this in Chapter 6). Tatyana Montyan, Kotsaba's lawyer, who managed to get him out of prison, has been of a similar opinion—the ongoing war, in her view, is a logical consequence of the Euromaidan, the Donbas war, and Kyiv's unwillingness to implement the Minsk agreements.

Establishing an "Anti-Russia" in Ukraine: An Engineered Disaster

Tatyana Montyan

Tatyana Montyan is a well-known Ukrainian lawyer and human rights activist. During the Euromaidan, she did not justify the government's violent actions against the demonstrators; however, she also opposed the ousting of President Yanukovych, arguing that it was unconstitutional.

In 2014, like Kotsaba, she visited Donbas and met with some field commanders of the anti-Maidan insurgents, covering the trip on her Facebook page. Following the visit, Montyan held a press conference and called for an immediate ceasefire and negotiations. Arguing that the conflict was a civil war, she stressed that the people of Donbas needed to be heard—not attacked by Ukrainian armed forces (Montyan, 2014). In 2015, when Kotsaba was arrested, Montyan gained notoriety for defending him as a lawyer (Montyan, 2015a). In December 2015, for "providing legal assistance to militants and participants in information attacks against Ukraine," she was placed on *Myrotvorets* (Montyan, 2015b). On February 10, 2023, the SSU charged Montyan of collaborating and encroaching on the territorial integrity of Ukraine. Currently, she resides in DNR and collects donations for local people through her blogs.

On February 19, 2022—five days before the current war started—Montyan addressed the Security Council of the United Nations, arguing that Ukraine "is the colony of the collective West . . . [where] . . . everything is decided by the people who came from the outside, who staged the Maidan and the coup d'état and took my country into slavery" (Montyan, 2022a, 6:27–36:42). These people, she claimed, "do not allow for the fulfillment of the Minsk agreements and will not allow doing this," because the true goal of the West, "despite all benevolent speeches . . . is to pit the Kiev regime against the republics and drag Russia into the war" (Montyan, 2022a, 6:42–47:05). Calling the Ukrainian government a "puppet regime" and the "marionettes" of the West, Montyan argued that Ukraine had been turned into "a chessboard, and the people of Ukraine and people in unrecognized republics are just a bargaining chip in geopolitical games" (Montyan, 2022a, 7:51–58:03).

For almost eight years, Montyan claimed, the Kiev regime had been shelling about 100,000 people with heavy artillery. PACE, nicknamed "blind observers" in those territories, did not react to this in any way. Montyan said she drove along the entire line of contact and saw with her own eyes that it was the civilian population that was being killed there: the most defenseless people who could not leave, including the elderly, the disabled, and women with children. In her presentation, all of Europe was looking on, "hypocritical and bloodthirsty," allowing people's suffering to continue for the eighth year while maintaining that the only possible solution was the Minsk agreements. "So, make your marionettes from the Kyiv regime fulfill them, or stop saying that there is no alternative," Montyan concluded (2022a, 8:37–10:08).

As is evident from her speech, Montyan, like Buzina, highlighted the link between the Maidan and "coup d'état," connected, in turn, to the "collective West," which was presented as "hypocritical" and "bloodthirsty." It is this "collective West," in Montyan's articulation, that turned Ukraine into a colony and a blood-soaked battlefield. Unlike Kotsaba, Montyan did not focus on the amorality of the Ukrainian political regime—as soon as Ukrainian political figures were labeled "marionettes" and "puppets," there was no sense in discussing their moral condition.

Montyan's address to the Security Council of the United Nations took place five days before the war started. In his address to the nation on the eve of the war, Putin (2022) also characterized SMO as a response to Ukraine systematically refusing to implement the Minsk agreements and said that Russia needed to stop the suffering of the Donbas people (Putin, 2022). Montyan's focus on Ukraine's "colonial status" with respect to the "collective West" was also in line with Putin's narrative about Ukraine's lack of independence and sovereignty. One might immediately assume that Montyan was nothing but a mouthpiece for Kremlin propaganda—a "collaborator," to put it in Zelensky's terms. The problem with this view of Montyan, based on her UN speech as well as her numerous other similar speeches on the subject, is that she had long been a critic not only of Kyiv's policies but also of Moscow's.

Starting in 2014, Montyan had been consistently criticizing the Kremlin for its conciliatory politics toward the post-Maidan government of Ukraine, its betrayal of Donbas due to unwillingness to go to war with Ukraine in 2014, and the stupidity of official Russian propaganda (e.g., Melnikov, 2022). Because of her frequent criticism of the Kremlin, one of the main Russian propagandists, Solovyov attacked Montyan personally. "Go to hell!" [подите вон] he shouted on his popular national show, accusing Montyan of insulting Putin and attempting to ruin Russia (Montyan, 2022b).

As mentioned earlier, there are many similar cases in which Ukrainians who hold anti-Maidan views have been attacked by promoters of Russia's official course. Anatoliy Sharij, one of the most popular Ukrainian bloggers now living in Spain, has also been steadily attacked by Russian hard-liners, but for a different reason—for the firm anti-war stance that he adopted after February 24 (Sharij, 2022a, 2022b).

Anatoliy Sharij

Prosecuted by the regime of then President Viktor Yanukovych for his publications related to Ukraine's corruption, oligarchy, and organized crime, Sharij found political asylum in the EU in 2012 (Cohen, 2022). In 2014, Sharij took a critical stance toward the Maidan's unconstitutional overturning of the government, which made him one of the top Ukrainian bloggers even though he was commenting on Ukrainian affairs from abroad (e.g., Sharij, 2014a). Because of his anti-Maidan position, Sharij was put on *Myrotvorets* in December 2014 (Sharij, 2014b).

In 2019, Sharij created from exile a center-right Libertarian political party, "The Party of Sharij," which actively supported Zelensky against Petro Poroshenko during the presidential campaign of 2019. Soon after Zelensky took office, however, Sharij realized that the new president was no better than the former one: the blogger argued that under Zelensky, corruption was going through the roof while radicalism and lawlessness flourished. Among his other investigations, Sharij made several programs on Zelensky's offshore accounts, which quickly made him persona non grata in Zelensky's Ukraine (Sharij, 2021b).

During Poroshenko's presidency, members of Sharij's party were frequently beaten, mutilated, and humiliated by radicals; this violence continued after Sharij joined the opposition against Zelensky (LB.ua, 2020; Sharij. net, 2021). In February 2021, the SSU charged Sharij with treason, accusing him of "spreading Russian propaganda." Numerous other criminal cases have been opened against Sharij; sanctions have been imposed not only against him but also against his close relatives (DOS, 2021, p. 26). On March 20, 2022, Sharij's party was banned by Zelensky's decree that prohibited all opposition parties, accusing them of connections with Russia.

Discussing the issue of external control over Ukraine, Sharij provides details about how the system of outside influences works. Claiming that "in

Ukraine, there are many organizations that exist exclusively for grant funds which are provided by [foreign] embassies . . . [and] . . . certain agencies directly connected with George Soros," Sharij argues that many Ukrainian so-called "activists" live exclusively on this money. Some of them, according to Sharij, have salaries from five to ten thousand dollars a month. "Ten thousand dollars in poor Ukraine, paid by organizations connected with Soros.[6] Why?" Sharij asks (Sharij, 2019, 0:05–11:07).

In answering this question, Sharij explains that in the aftermath of the Euromaidan revolution, under "Poroshenko's regime," there were "reform offices" added to each ministry and staffed by employees who received their salaries from foreign grants. The main goal of these "reform offices" has been to work out neoliberal reforms—such as Ukraine's deforestation or the sales of national land resources—or reforms in public administration, "to select public prosecutors, for example," as Sharij (2019, 8:10–18:14) claims.[7]

According to Sharij, not only have these offices remained in operation during Zelensky's presidency, but their former heads have gone on to join the government as deputy ministers. Following the instructions of foreign "advisors," these corrupted governmental officials "draw up a bill and give it to the ministry, [and then] the ministry submits this bill [to the parliament] on its behalf" (Sharij, 2019, 12:14–12:25). "Guys, we have to fight this external government of Ukraine," concluded Sharij (2019, 12:46–12:48), who can still fight against it, though only from abroad.

As mentioned in the introductory part of the book, I analyzed all of Sharij's Telegram posts from February 24 until March 20. My analysis shows that he did not welcome Russia's special military operation, and he was particularly indignant over Russia's shelling of residential areas in Ukraine (Sharij, 2022a). From the first day of the war, Sharij used his YouTube channel to help Ukrainians in distress: "to find lost relatives, to help the elderly, the sick, people with disabilities, children and everyone in need" (Sharij, 2022e). So when Sharij's Facebook and YouTube accounts became inaccessible in Ukraine (on February 27 and March 7, respectively), this took away a chance for many people to receive much-needed help. "A coward [крыса] posing as a great hero, hiding in a bunker and taking his wife and children out of the country in advance, is depriving people of the opportunity to save their children"[8]— such was Sharij's harsh depiction of Zelensky after the channels were blocked within Ukraine (Sharij, 2022d).

Sharij was very critical of Zelensky, saying he engaged in "self-promotion against the background of people dying of starvation in the basements near Kyiv" (Sharij, 2022f) and that his officials had failed to prepare evacuation plans. Before the invasion, Sharij maintained, Zelensky kept persuading people that there would be no attack while Western intelligence argued otherwise (Sharij, 2022a, 15:18–15:22). Later, this was confirmed by Joe Biden who claimed that Zelensky "did not want to hear" warnings of Russia's invasion (Ambrose, 2022).

Sharij has also been outraged by the crackdown on opposition figures (Sharij, 2022b); he has been writing about the extrajudicial killings of "traitors," citing, for example, the case of Denis Kireev, one of the negotiators at the first Gomel meeting[9] who was killed "right in the center of Kyiv" (Sharij, 2022c) as a warning to other collaborators (Forrest, 2023).[10]

As should be clear from all these examples, in Sharij's representation, the chain of equivalence characterizing the post-Maidan government in Ukraine, including under Zelensky, comprises nodal points such as external control and corruption (linked to neoliberal reforms, foreign granting foundations, reform offices, and foreign-bankrolled activists who shape legislation), radicalism and lawlessness, persecution of dissent, extrajudicial killings, abductions, and so forth. In his presentation, the ongoing war in Ukraine is linked to both Russian and Ukrainian war crimes and propaganda, human suffering, and the amorality of government power—its hypocrisy, self-promotion, lack of care for people, and lack of professionalism. What unites Sharij's discursive constructions with those of Montyan and Buzina is that Sharij also emphasizes the external control over Ukraine; what unites him with Kotsaba is his focus on the amorality of Zelensky's system of power. Even though Sharij does not support Russia's SMO while Montyan does, both have faced backlash not only from the Ukrainian government but also from Russian hard-liners and official propagandists (Sharij, 2022g, 2022h).

Dmitry Vasilets

Dmitry Vasilets came to journalism from a software business with an idea of fighting against media propaganda that provokes civil confrontations. He used his own funds to launch several journalistic projects such as the *Museum of Information War*, in which he analyzed current events from different perspectives, revealing propagandistic media tricks and criticizing media for pitting Ukrainians against each other (*MIW*, 2014). Vasilets also organized the movement "Media Lustration," which was supposed to monitor media outlets and hold accountable those inciting war through lies and propaganda; he and his fellows also founded a journalistic anti-award named after Nazi propagandist Joseph Goebbels to shame the worst offenders (Vasilets, 2017).

After Vasilets—like Montyan and Kotsana—visited Donbas in the summer of 2014 to see the situation for himself, he was accused of supporting terrorism. On November 24, 2015, Vasilets was arrested; five days later, his name appeared on *Myrotvorets* (Vasilets, 2015). In 2017, a Ukrainian court sentenced him to nine years in prison on charges of treason and complicity in terrorism (Council of Europe, 2018). He had been held for a total of two years and three months by the time of his release under house arrest on February 21, 2018. The following year, Vasilets assumed the leadership of "Derzhava," a socialist political party that was banned along with ten other oppositional parties through an NSDC decision in March 2022. Soon after Russia started its

SMO, Vasilets was able to leave the country; he currently produces his video blogs from abroad (his exact whereabouts are unknown).

For the purposes of this book, I have selected his YouTube video uploaded on January 27, 2022, in which he discussed the "unending series of [neoliberal] reforms which began immediately after the formation of the new post-Maidan Cabinet of Ministers" (Vasilets, 2022a, 0:20–30:25).[11] According to Vasilets, the main neoliberal reform that has changed the financial, economic, and social structures of Ukraine has been the transition to the market system of price formation for all energy resources, including gas. Even though Ukraine meets 70 percent of its gas needs through its own production, post-Maidan reforms have resulted in Ukrainians having to pay market prices established in the Netherlands as well as the costs of gas delivery. Not only has the new system of price formation caused increased tariffs for housing and communal services, higher costs for all domestic products, and a lower standard of living for Ukrainians, but it also kills the nation's industry, Vasilets (2022a) argued.

Vasilets also reminded his audience how, in response to the de-industrialization of Ukraine—a direct consequence of the Euromaidan—the West, as represented by then US Ambassador Geoffrey Pyatt (2016), promised that Ukraine would become an "agrarian superpower." However, Ukraine has been transformed instead into an exporter of agricultural products with minimal added value. A developed industrial and agrarian state under the Soviet rule, Ukraine turned into an importer of basic agricultural products including meat and even vegetables, Vasilets lamented, explaining that "it is simply not profitable for farmers to grow carrots, onions, and beets amid high demand, rising prices for grains and oilseeds" (Vasilets, 2022a, 6:15–16:22). Once the government ceased to regulate this market, Vasilets claimed, "the flip side of excessive profits for Ukrainian exporters of cereals and oilseeds is excessive costs for ordinary Ukrainians" (Vasilets, 2022a, 6:33–36:40).

The general impoverishment caused by post-Maidan neoliberal reforms brought a record level of labor migration of Ukrainians to European countries: "According to the National Bank of Ukraine, for 11 months of 2021, labor migrants sent more than $14 billion to Ukraine, which is almost 20 percent more than in the whole of 2020," Vasilets maintained (2022a, 7:12–17:26). Because young and qualified workers made up the bulk of those leaving for jobs in Europe, "Ukraine is losing incentives to develop domestic production," he argued (Vasilets, 2022a, 8:45–48:50). "The EU's business plan, called 'Euromaidan' or the 'Revolution of Dignity'—you may call this as you like—turned out to be super profitable," Vasilets concluded (2022a, 9:38–39:47).

As is evident from these excerpts, for Vasilets, the Euromaidan was linked primarily to the establishment of external control over Ukraine in the sphere of neoliberal reforms, de-industrialization, rising cost of living, a declining standard of living, impoverishment, and labor migration. Unlike Buzina and Montyan, who connected external rule over Ukraine with the country's transformation into a pawn in the geopolitical games of the West and the human suffering related to the Donbas war, Vasilets (in the piece under analysis) emphasizes the connections between external control and its detrimental socioeconomic impacts for Ukrainians due to the neoliberal overhaul of economic relations. In his articulations, Vasilets is closer to Sharij, though the former is more concerned with the impoverishment of Ukraine's people while the latter focuses on the loss of Ukraine's national sovereignty in the economic sphere.

Like Montyan (and in contrast to Kotsaba and Sharij), Vasilets (2022b) welcomed the beginning of Russia's SMO. "Who favors the war?" he asked rhetorically, and answered himself:

> No one! Who needed all this? Destroyed cities, torn families, tens of thousands dead, millions of impoverished migrants, refugees? No one! But who needed a coup d'état in 2014? . . . Who needed to announce an ATO in the spring of 2014 and send armed columns to Mariupol, Slavyansk, Kramatorsk, Donetsk [Donbas cities]? Who did it in such a way that it became dangerous to be Russian in Ukraine? . . . Who hid in prisons those to whom the Russian language, Russian culture, historical friendship with Russia were close in spirit?

According to Vasilets, the war started "because Russia's repeated proposals . . . to agree on providing the Russians in Ukraine with minimum conditions for a decent existence and development, and joint security rules with NATO and the United States, led to nothing" (Vasilets, 2022b). In his view, those responsible for the Maidan and further escalation of the situation—NATO and the United States—had done nothing to prevent the ongoing war.

Conclusion

In this chapter, I discussed five of Ukraine's famous anti-Maidan figures whose discursive constructions help to destabilize the post-Maidan hegemonic discourse endorsed by Zelensky. Despite the differences in their individual cases, all of them show that the Euromaidan, the Donbas war, and the ongoing conflict can be articulated in terms of external control and national sovereignty, neoliberalism and social justice, radicalism and inclusive coexistence, nationalism and cultural diversity, authoritarianism and freedom of opinion, and so on. Only if such alternative perspectives are included in our analysis of the situation can we hope to understand its complexity. Moreover, for even the beginnings of a peaceful solution to materialize, it is essential to move away from dichotomization, make the solid frontiers between the self and the other more porous, and foster pluralism of opinions and positions. The following chapters will provide further elaboration.

Notes

1 "Hohol" is a derogatory term to denote Ukrainians. Although it is now considered offensive, the term was rather common in Gogol's times.
2 The Berkut was a special police force holding back the onslaught of protesters during the Euromaidan. The majority of the Berkut officers in service during the clashes were from the southeastern parts of Ukraine (Wilson, 2014, p. 75).
3 As I explain in Chapter 1, millions of Ukrainians who supported the Euromaidan were sure they were struggling for a better democratic future. However, their progressive aspirations had nothing to do with the aims of Ukrainian nationalists and their supporters in the fight to overthrow the government.
4 Thirty of Zelensky's old friends and acquaintances received state positions after Zelensky came to power, according to the Committee of Voters (2020).
5 95th Quarter is the title of Zelensky's studio producing comedies.
6 In Ukraine, it is widely believed that George Soros and his "sorosyata"—a popular meme in Ukrainian political discourse denoting grant-receiving individuals and organizations—represent the interests of global neoliberal institutions (Demyachuk, 2021).
7 Mustafa Nayem, who helped to initiate the Euromaidan (see Chapter 1), can serve as a good example to illustrate how the scheme described by Sharij works. In 2019, Nayem, despite lacking adequate professional experience, was appointed Deputy Director General of Ukroboronprom—a conglomerate of multiproduct enterprises in various sectors of Ukraine's defense industry. In 2021, he was appointed Deputy Minister of Infrastructure of Ukraine.
8 According to Sharij (2022h), Zelensky's family, along with the families of other officials, was evacuated before Kyiv was bombed; later, when Russian troops retreated from the capital, his wife returned.
9 The first round of negotiations with Russia after the beginning of the war.
10 Kireev was reportedly executed on suspicion of being a Russian spy.
11 Vasilets' YouTube channels were blocked in January 2023.

Reference List

Aleks Orange. (2019, October 29). Zelensky received a summons and evaded the summons (In Russian). *YouTube*. www.youtube.com/watch?v=FzFQIQek-GM

Ambrose, T. (2022, June 11). Zelenskiy 'didn't want to hear' warnings of Russia invasion, says Biden. *Guardian*. www.theguardian.com/world/2022/jun/11/volodymyr-zelenskiy-didnt-want-to-hear-warnings-of-russia-invasion-says-joe-biden

Amnesty International. (2015, April 17). *Ukraine's spate of suspicious deaths must be followed by credible investigations*. www.amnesty.org/en/latest/news/2015/04/ukraine-suspicious-deaths-need-credible-investigations/

Buzina, O. (2009, April 28). Oles Buzina wants to jail Nazi (in Russian). *Segodnya*. https://ukraine.segodnya.ua/ukraine/olec-buzina-khochet-cazhat-natsictov-159109.html

Buzina, O. (2014, January 30). Oles Buzyna vs Vladimir Zhirynovsky in Vladimir Solovyov's talk show "Duel" (in Russian). *YouTube*. www.youtube.com/watch?v=1H65fWYoaV8

Buzina, O. (2015, April 16). I don't like this version of Ukraine (In Russian). *Russian People's Line*. https://ruskline.ru/analitika/2015/12/23/ya_ne_lyublyu_takuyu_ukrainu

Chambers, F., & Freedom, T. (2022, April 13). Ukrainian refuseniks on why many won't fight for Ukraine. *Popular Resistance*. https://popularresistance.org/ukrainian-refuseniks-on-why-many-wont-fight-for-ukraine/?fbclid=IwAR1RtVBVrZOai-Xxw7TQbhPXKQPF2aJW-tYTFLrOI32Tzk8Vq6uevg0Qrpo&mibextid=ATveJy

Cohen, D. (2022, April 14). Testimony reveals Zelensky's secret police plot to "liquidate" opposition figure Anatoly Shariy. *Mint Press News*. www.mintpressnews.
com/volodymyr-zelensky-secret-police-hunted-down-opposition-anatoly-shariy/280200

Committee of Voters. (2020, May 15). *During one year, more than 30 members of "Kvartal 95"
took public positions* (in Ukrainian). www.cvu.org.ua/nodes/view/type:news/slug:za-
rik-na-derzhavnykhposadakh-opyn ylysia-ponad-30-kvartalivtsiv-i-ikh-znaiomykh

Council of Europe. (2018, March 28). Two Ukrainian journalists sentenced to 9 years'
imprisonment for assisting separatism. *Safety of Journalists Platform*. https://fom.
coe.int/en/alerte/detail/32000740

Council of Europe. (2021, September 2). *Ukrainian journalist Ruslan Kotsaba attacked
with chemical substance*. https://fom.coe.int/en/alerte/detail/102265091;globalSear
ch=true

Demyachuk, T. (2021, January 25). "Sorosyata" and "external governance" of Ukraine:
A conspiracy narrative fueling anti-Western discourse. *European Security Journal*.
www.esjnews.com/sorosyata-and-external-governa

Deutsche Welle. (2018, November 15). Gerhard Schröder labeled "enemy of the
state" in Ukraine. *DW.com*. www.dw.com/en/gerhard-schr%C3%B6der-labeled-
enemy-of-the-state-in-ukraine/a-46319939

DOS. (2016). Ukraine 2016 human rights report. *State Department*. www.state.gov/
wp-content/uploads/2017/03/Ukraine-Crimea.pdf

DOS. (2021). Ukraine 2021 human rights report. *State Department*. www.state.
gov/wp-content/uploads/2022/04/313615_UKRAINE-2021-HUMAN- RIGHTS-
REPORT.pdf

Forrest, B. (2023, January 18). Russian spy or Ukrainian hero? The strange death
of Denys Kiryeyev. *Wall Street Journal*. www.wsj.com/articles/russian-spy-or-
ukrainian-hero-the-strange-death-of-denys-kiryeyev-11674059395

Kotsaba, R. (2014, June 14). Journalist Ruslan Kotsaba about his stay in the ATO zone
(In Ukrainian). *YouTube*. www.youtube.com/watch?v=ICUonUirmwM

Kotsaba, R. (2015, January 17). Internet campaign "I refuse mobilization" (in Ukrainian). *YouTube*. www.youtube.com/watch?v=Ve_AJRn-HJA&t=4s

Kotsaba, R. (2016, March 16). Kotsaba Ruslan Petrovych (in Ukrainian). *Myrotvorets*.
https://myrotvorets.center/criminal/kocaba-ruslan-petrovich/

Kotsaba, R. (2022, February 18). Video appeal to Volodymyr Zelensky, a former comedian and the current President of Ukraine (in Ukrainian). *YouTube*. www.youtube.
com/watch?v=61Hknuhn2yA

LB.ua. (2020, June 25). *In Kharkov, a member of Shariy's party is severely beaten*
(in Russian). https://rus.lb.ua/society/2020/06/25/460635_harkove_zhestoko_izbili.
html

Melnikov, R. (2022, October 22). Fights without rules. Lawyer Tatyana Montyan
spoke about the special operation and life in Donetsk (in Russian). *RGRU*. https://
rg.ru/2022/10/22/boi-bez-pravil-advokat-tatiana-montian-rasskazala-ob-svo-i-zhiz
ni-v-donecke.html

MIV. (2014, December 11). Promo "Information Warfare Museum" (In Russian).
https://www.youtube.com/watch?v=BduviqvUzgM

Montyan, T. (2014, December 10). Press conference: "Humanitarian disaster in Donbas" (in Ukrainian). *YouTube*. www.youtube.com/watch?v=RDnBx2GYOh4

Montyan, T. (2015a, September 24). Tatyana Montyan about the case of Ruslan Kotsaba,
accused of treason (in Ukrainian). www.youtube.com/watch?v=7PQQrzK8oLs

Montyan, T. (2015b, December 8). Montyan Tatyana Nilolaevna (in Russian). *Myrotvorets*. https://myrotvorets.center/criminal/montyan-tatyana-nikolaevna/

Montyan, T. (2020, November 26). Maidan as a political technology for a coup d'état (in Russian). *YouTube*. www.youtube.com/watch?v=IcPLmGA5DRU

Montyan, T. (2022a, February 19). Scandal in the UN Security Council. War in Ukraine. Speech by Tatyana Montyan (in Russian). *YouTube*. www.youtube.com/watch?v=V9Ds_UZ8Ifs

Montyan, T. (2022b, June 30). Who are you, Montyan, to teach me?! (in Russian). *Telegram*. https://t.me/montyan2/1774

Plokhy, S. (2008). *Ukraine and Russia: Representations of the past*. Toronto: University of Toronto Press.

Putin, V. (2022, February 21). Address by the President of the Russian Federation (in Russian). *Kremlin*. http://en.kremlin.ru/events/president/news/67828

Pyatt, G. (2016, February 24). U.S. Ambassador: The Ukrainian Government has demonstrated real progress to make it possible for American agricultural companies to come to Ukraine. *Government Portal*. www.kmu.gov.ua/en/news/248855206

Radio Liberty. (2019, April 13). *The ministry of defense said whether presidential candidate Zelensky served in the army* (in Ukrainian). www.radiosvoboda.org/a/news-u-minoborony-rozpovily-chy-sluzhyv-v-armii-zelenskyy/29879219.html

Reuters. (2015, April 16). *Ukrainian journalist with pro-Russian views shot dead in Kiev*. www.reuters.com/article/ukraine-crisis-crime-idINKBN0N718720150416

Sharij, A. (2014a, March 20). The rifle that Pashinsky took away (in Russian). *From-ua.com*. https://from-ua.com/articles/303923-a-sharii-vintovka-kotoruyu-vivez-pashinskii-dokumenti-i-fakti.html

Sharij, A. (2014b, December 14). Sharij Anatolij Anatolyevich (in Russian). *Myrotvorets*. https://myrotvorets.center/criminal/sharij-anatolij-anatolevich

Sharij, A. (2019, November 24). On the external rule (in Russian). *YouTube*. www.youtube.com/watch?v=TZ9iOHPHg5g

Sharij, A. (2021a, July 3). Zelensky: "Russians and Ukrainians are one nation" (in Russian). *YouTube*. www.youtube.com/watch?v=cVxtAnrJ73w&t=5s

Sharij, A. (2021b, October 4). Zelensky fights off offshore accusations (in Russian). *YouTube*. www.youtube.com/watch?v=wTZ4kBcpQlY

Sharij, A. (2022a, February 24). The invasion (in Russian). *YouTube*. www.youtube.com/watch?v=7gO6vuI2-BQ

Sharij, A. (2022b, February 27). Still wondering how it turns out (in Russian). *Telegram*. https://t.me/ASupersharij/8643

Sharij, A. (2022c, March 5). The negotiator at the first Gomel meeting of Kireev was actually killed (in Russian). *Telegram*. https://t.me/ASupersharij/8704

Sharij, A. (2022d, March 7). Well, install a VPN, friends (in Russian). *Telegram*. https://t.me/ASupersharij/8716

Sharij, A. (2022e, March 12). For 16 days, Shariy has been streaming days and nights (in Russian). *Telegram*. https://t.me/ASupersharij/8769

Sharij, A. (2022f, March 17). Didn't he leave? (in Russian). *Telegram*. https://t.me/ASupersharij/8831

Sharij, A. (2022g, November 19). Yesterday, I told one man . . . (in Russian). *Telegram*. https://t.me/ASupersharij/13234

Sharij, A. (2022h, November 21). Do you know what the Russian government wants? (in Russian). *Telegram*. https://t.me/ASupersharij/13274

Sharij.net. (2021, May 10). *In Lviv, on the victory day, a supporter of Sharij's party was beaten* (in Russian). https://sharij.net/vo-lvove-izbili-storonnika-partii-shariya-video

UN OHCHR. (2018, February 15). *Report on the human rights situation in Ukraine.* Office of the United Nations High Commissioner for Human Rights. www.ohchr.org/documents/Countries/uA/reportukraineNov2017-Feb2018_eN.pdf

Wilson, A. (2014). *Ukraine crisis: What it means for the West.* Yale University Press.

Vasilets, D. (2015, November 11). Vasilets Dmitry Andreevich (in Russian). *Myrotvorets.* https://myrotvorets.center/criminal/vasilec-dmitrij-andreevich/

Vasilets, D. (2017, October 11). Letter from Dmitry Vasilets. *Stalkzone.* www.stalkerzone.org/letter-dmitry-vasilets-no-kind-uncles-us-eu-dream-helping-u kraine/

Vasilets, D. (2022a, January 27). Dmitry Vasilets on reforms in Ukraine (in Russian). *YouTube.* www.youtube.com/watch?v=FtcZvgaeYE

Vasilets, D. (2022b, November 26). Who favors the war? (in Russian). *Telegram.* https://t.me/VasiletsDmitriy/5695

Zelensky, V. (2022a, April 5). President of Ukraine Volodymyr Zelensky addressed the people and politicians of Spain (in Ukrainian). *YouTube.* www.youtube.com/watch?v=AXPdGxwtIsU

Zelensky, V. (2022b, May 3). Volodymyr Zelensky addressed the people and politicians of Albania (in Ukrainian). *YouTube.* www.youtube.com/watch?v=s1bIIb1AlEA

5 Authoritarian Populism in the Name of Democracy

The Impossible Unity of Ukraine

As the previous chapters demonstrate, the unity of Ukraine, which Zelensky constantly invokes in his war speeches, has been established not only discursively but also through the physical exclusion of oppositional voices from the public sphere of Ukraine. These acts of repression started not with the onset of war between Russia and Ukraine in 2022 but much earlier, after the victory of the Maidan in 2014 and the beginning of the Donbas war. One of the most decisive points separating pre-Maidan and post-Maidan times in terms of the radicalization of the internal societal split was the tragedy in Odessa, a Russian-speaking city located on the Black Sea, where on May 2, 2014, 48 people died after street clashes between two groups of Ukrainians on opposing sides of the Maidan revolution (Baysha, 2020c).

The brief account of the tragedy provided here is based on the investigations conducted by the United Nations (UN OHCHR, 2014) and the Council of Europe (2015). The clashes started in the afternoon, after a pro-Maidan rally of soccer fans whose teams were playing that day in Odessa skirmished with anti-Maidan activists; it was the anti-Maidan side that attacked the pro-Maidan rally first. The rally quickly turned into a violent confrontation during which six people were shot dead and dozens were wounded. Toward evening, the pro-Maidan side took the offensive and chased the anti-Maidan group in retreat to its base camp at Kulikovo Field, a square near the House of Trade Union. There, the former burned the tents of the latter. The anti-Maidan protesters found shelter in the House of Trade Union, from where they hurled Molotov cocktails at the pro-Maidan group; their adversaries retaliated in kind. One of the bottles containing flammable liquid is presumed to have struck a barricade, igniting a fire that quickly engulfed the union building. Forty-two people died in the incident, including those who burned to death or suffocated, and others who fell from high windows in the blaze, while more than 200 survivors were left with burns and other injuries.

According to a United Nations report, "some 'Pro-Unity' [pro-Maidan] protesters were beating up 'Pro-Federalism' [anti-Maidan] supporters as

DOI: 10.4324/9781003379164-8

they were trying to escape the Trade Union Building, while others were trying to help them" (UN OHCHR, 2014, p. 10). However, for those holding anti-Maidan views, the tragedy acquired the meaning of a mass killing that had been done on purpose, in line with promises to "kill *koloradi*," a phrase spread by pro-Maidan media and on social networks leading up to the tragedy (Baysha, 2020b). *Kolorad* is a word originally denoting Colorado potato-eating insects distinctive for their bright orange-and-black stripes. Because their colors are reminiscent of the orange-and-black St. George ribbon, a symbol of Russian military glory, the term came to denote Maidan opponents, equated to pro-Russian activists.

In April 2014, it was popular among pro-Maidan users of social media to share posters featuring alerts about the presence of *koloradi* in the cities of southeastern Ukraine and advocating for their extermination (Baysha, 2020a). The day the tragedy occurred, pro-Maidan social networks were full of posts that cheered the victory over *koloradi*. Here are some immediate reactions posted by members of the EuroMaydan (2014) group on Facebook: "extinguish koloradi!"; "kill koloradi!"; "koloradi bugs need to be burnt!"; "to burn all koloradi!"; "death to koloradi!"; and so forth. These and similar posts indicate that the Odessa tragedy was not simply a horrible accident, no matter whose actions caused the clashes and the fire: When the level of animosity between compatriots is so high, violence of such scale and intensity is highly probable.

In Ukrainian propaganda, the Odessa tragedy appeared exclusively as an external provocation (Segodnya, 2014a)—part of Russia's plan to split Ukraine (Censor, 2014a), which had been prepared by the Kremlin's secret service (Gordon, 2014). It was implied that Russia was attempting to destroy the unity of the Ukrainian state, where "no confrontation among people exists" (ICTV, 2014). As in Zelensky's efforts in the current war between Russia and Ukraine to create an impression that his country has been a homogeneous unity existing beyond social divides, these propagandistic constructions of the Odessa tragedy reduced the complexity of the situation to a monistic and deterministic explanation solely in terms of Russia's actions.

The day after the tragedy, most Ukrainian media were quick to disseminate the claim that most of the participants of the mass disorder are the citizens of Russia and Transdnistria (Segodnya, 2014b). It was reported that among the victims, there are 15 Russians and five Transdnistrians (TSN, 2014), 15 Russians and ten Transdnistrians (Censor, 2014b), and so forth. These figures were completely fake, but spread rapidly through social networks nonetheless. Every victim of the street clashes and fire on May 2, 2014, in Odessa was later identified as Ukrainian: "According to various sources, all those who died were Ukrainian citizens" (UN OHCHR, 2014, p. 10).

The reduction of the internal social complexity of the situation has been achieved by excluding alternative visions from the public sphere of Ukraine. However, there have been some journalists who—at the expense of coming under surveillance by the security services—went on propagating independent views. One of them is Yuri Tkachev, a journalist from Odessa who lost some of his anti-Maidan comrades in the fire. He transformed the local newspaper *Timer* into a public platform where silenced outlooks could be presented. With the beginning of the Russia–Ukraine war of 2022, *Timer* was banned and Tkachev was arrested (Yasinsky, 2022).

Yuri Tkachev[1]

Among the anti-Maidan community, Tkachev is known nationwide for his harsh criticism of the nationalistic policies of the post-Maidan governments and his activities to protect freedom of speech and the human rights of Russian speakers. He was also a member of the "May 2" group, an independent commission of Odessa journalists and civil society representatives whose investigation of the tragedy was cited in UN reports (UN OHCHR, 2014). Since 2014, Tkachev had been under SSU surveillance (Tkachev, 2022a). On March 11, 2022, he was arrested by the SSU on weapons charges: illegal possession of weapons and explosives (Wilayto, 2022). According to Tkachev, the SSU planted the weapons during the search of his house (Sharij, 2022). Three months later, on June 9, 2022, he was released on bail; since that day, Tkachev has not been reporting, and it is unclear if he is still free.

On the eve of Russia's invasion of Ukraine, on February 23, 2022, Tkachev made a Telegram post in which he responded to those criticizing him for not supporting Ukraine. Tkachev argued that all his life he tried to be an exemplary citizen, which did not prevent him from getting the status of an enemy of the state. He admitted that he had been more fortunate than Buzina, his friend who died on May 2, or those who spent years in Ukrainian prisons. "But if you seriously think that surveillance, wiretapping and fabricated criminal cases contribute to the growth of sympathy for the state, then you are mistaken," he argued (Tkachev, 2022a). He also reminded his critics that in Ukraine, there were regular public statements that people with his views should be silenced, expelled from the country, or even killed. Tkachev could not recall a single instance of anyone being held accountable for such statements, which, in his view, meant that the Ukrainian government shared the same opinion, or at least did not object to it. The state was intentionally forcing Russian language and culture to the margins of social and cultural life, Tkachev maintained, arguing that state-funded educational institutions were promoting hostile attitudes toward Russian speakers with propaganda that portrayed them as second-class citizens.

"All these years it was not Russia that has been threatening me and people like me with deprivation of citizenship, deportation, camps, prison, and murder," Tkachev (2022a) claimed. It was not Russia, he argued, that killed and imprisoned Ukrainian citizens, including his friends, for wrong views, and it was not Russia using gangs of "activists" controlled by special services to intimidate "others." Addressing his critics, Tkachev asked them to give at least one reason for him to be on the side of Ukraine in this situation. "To protect it so it can continue to humiliate and oppress people like me? Sorry, masochism is not my thing. It should be enough for Ukraine that in the current situation I will not participate in the war on my own, informational front from the opposite side," Tkachev (2022a) maintained.

Tkachev's arrest on March 11 came a little more than two weeks after the beginning of the current war. As my analysis of his war-related posts shows, Tkachev blamed Ukraine for non-implementation of the Minsk agreements, which, in his opinion, led to the war (Tkachev, 2022b). He also drew parallels between the shelling of Ukrainian cities in 2022 and what had been happening in Donbas since 2014: "Well, we do understand—don't we?—that Donbas has been feeling what we are now feeling for the last eight years" (Tkachev, 2022c).

In his war-related posts, Tkachev criticized the Ukrainian authorities for locating troops in residential areas; for publishing pictures of Russian soldiers who had been captured or killed; for producing fake videos; and especially for prosecuting and executing "collaborators" and "traitors." Commenting on Zelensky's statement that the abducting by Russian forces of the mayor of Melitopol is a war crime against democracy, Tkachev inquired: "Do you want to comment on the murder of Kremennaya Mayor Vladimir Struk? [2] And what about Dzhangirov, Dudin, and other bloggers [arrested after February 24, 2022]?" (Tkachev, 2022h).

Given that many "anti-Maidan others" did not welcome Russia's SMO, it was astonishing for Tkachev that the Ukrainian authorities continued to repress them even after February 24, when many pro-Russian Ukrainians started seeing Russia in a negative light (Tkachev, 2022e). Under the pretext of war, the information space is being cleaned of all speakers disloyal to the authorities, regardless of what position they have chosen in relation to the war, he asserted (Tkachev, 2022g). Commenting on the arrest of one of the members of Sharij's party, Tkachev highlighted the fact that Sharij fully supported Ukraine, which, however, did not save his people from repression. He suggested that those in power are simply taking revenge for past grievances (Tkachev, 2022j).

As is evident from this brief account of his posts, Tkachev—like Montyan, Vasilets, and Kotsaba—linked the current war to Ukraine's "anti-terrorist operation" in Donbas and the non-implementation by Kyiv of the Minsk agreements. But his major concern was the violation of human rights in Ukraine. He articulated the post-Maidan regime by linking it to surveillance, fabricated criminal cases, unjust imprisonment, extrajudicial executions, intimidation, and "gangs of 'activists'" directed by Ukraine's special services and allowed to commit crimes with impunity. The post-Maidan system of government was also articulated by Tkachev through linkages to radical nationalism: hostile attitudes toward Russian language and culture, and the treatment of Russian speakers as second-class citizens.

Notably, even with the strength of his negative attitude toward the Ukrainian authorities and his belief that they were to blame for the war—"to be honest, I am overwhelmed with stupid black hatred for those who brought this . . ."—Zelensky/Poroshenko/Biden" (Tkachev, 2022d)—Tkachev was also critical toward Russia, condemning its shelling of residential areas and calling these acts war crimes (Tkachev, 2022f). He was also very critical of Russia's propaganda for identifying all active pro-Ukrainian citizens and the Ukrainian military as Nazis, which, in his view, was an ugly distortion of the real situation (Tkachev, 2022i).

Although such criticism of Russia could hardly be considered collaboration with the enemy—the charge with which Zelensky dismissed journalists who, in his view, "spread lies" about the war (i.e., did not reproduce the official Ukrainian propaganda)—Tkachev could not avoid arrest. The same fate awaited many other Ukrainians who believed that Ukraine was at least partially responsible for the ongoing war.

Journalists as Enemies of the People

As illustrated by the stories of Buzina, Kotsaba, Montyan, Sharij, Vasilets, and Tkachev, the prosecution of oppositional journalists presented as "enemies of the people" started long before the eruption of the current war. The beginning of Russia's "special military operation" just marked another level of efforts to crush dissent. On March 20, 2022, Zelensky signed a decision by the National Security and Defense Council (NSDC) to ban 11 oppositional political parties, justifying the move in an address to the nation with the pretext of their links to the Russian aggressor (Zelensky, 2022a). Along with banning the parties, Zelensky also implemented the NSDC decision to launch a telethon called "United News #UARAZOM," which all national TV channels were expected to broadcast.

Explaining these decisions to the nation, Zelensky highlighted the importance of a "unified information policy" under martial law (IMI, 2022). The problem with this formulation, however, is that Zelensky's policy of silencing the opposition started in February 2021 (see Introduction), well before the ongoing war. In his address to the nation on the decision to shut down the first three oppositional channels, Zelensky described the banned media as "talking armies lying and zombifying people very professionally" (Zelensky, 2021, 9:50–59:56):

> There are mass media, and there are weapons of mass destruction. . . . Information projectiles strike the mind. . . . There is freedom of speech, and there are words that can lead to non-freedom. . . . There is criticism against individuals, and there is sabotage against the country.
>
> (15:09–15:36)

"Only a truthful word should be free," Zelensky argued (2021, 15:25–15:27). To cement the mendacity of oppositional channels in the eyes of the nation, the president dubbed them corrupted media (Zelensky, 2021, 0:33–40:37) in the pocket of powerful manipulators (literally, "pocket channels"). In Zelensky's view, they "poured into people's ears endless streams of lies" (Zelensky, 2021, 1:01–11:08) that were "arrogant, cynical, and most important, dangerous" (Zelensky, 2021, 6:01–6:06). Those who did not "want to get a portion of such juicy and perfect nonsense for lunch" (Zelensky, 2021, 0:37–40:45) should not listen to these channels, Zelensky argued.

In Zelensky's view, it would be better if, instead of swallowing the information poison of the opposition, Ukrainians would turn to their president, who had been directly and fairly informing them about governmental work and the victories of Ukraine (Zelensky, 2021, 0:46–50:52) without media distortions. In contrast to the fake-news channels spreading "delirium on a cosmic scale," as Zelensky (2021, 3:35–43:36) put it, he was ready to discuss with his nation everything in detail: openly and honestly (Zelensky, 2021, 6:40–46:45).

One year later, thanks to the war with Russia, Zelensky was able to turn this idea into reality: Ukrainian media had little choice but to show daily presidential speeches and the telethon "United News #UARAZOM," which reflects the "only true" version of events. All oppositional (i.e., "lying") journalists and bloggers had to either shut up (voluntarily or under duress) or, if possible, emigrate. Taras Nezalezhko—a "social rapper," as he called himself—was among the latter.

Taras Nezalezhko

Taras Nezalezhko is a musician from Kyiv who became well-known in 2015 after releasing his song "Jump, bitch!"—a sarcastic reflection on the popular chant among Maidan protesters, "If you are not jumping, you are a *moskal.*" As explained in Chapter 1, in the representation of anti-Maidan Ukrainians, including Nezalezhko, the signifier "jumpers" came to denote all Maidan protesters, who were cast as childish or infantile. "Do not think with your head, shout your chants," Nezalezhko's song goes:

> Break everything that someone has already built for you
> Merge in frenzied ecstasy with the dirty crowd.
> You are in search of enemies, the Kremlin's hand . . .
> But, bitch, you should have started with yourself!
> (Nezalezhko, 2015)

Other compositions by Nezalezhko, popular among anti-Maidan Ukrainians, were also related to Ukraine's post-Maidan times. He ridiculed Ukrainian politics, advocated for peace, and called for a democratic change in songs such as "I choose peace," "Immortal regiment,"[3] "Democracy," and others.

Apart from singing, Nezalezhko tried his hand at political blogging with videos on his YouTube channel. Among the various oppositional speakers Nezalezhko hosted, a permanent guest in his studio was Dmitry Dzhangirov, who was arrested on March 8, 2022 (see Chapter 6). Without waiting for his own arrest, Nezalezhko managed to flee Ukraine, an account of which appeared on his YouTube channel several days later. Addressing his followers, Nezalezhko informed them that he was no longer in the country and that he had rather mixed feelings about this. The first feeling was joy, because after almost 40 days of staying in Kyiv since the beginning of the war, he was able to leave Ukraine. The negative feeling was helplessness, because he could not help many of his friends who were by then "in the dungeons of the Ukrainian gestapo," as Nezalezhko put it (2022a, 0:15–20:45).[4]

Nezalezhko advised his supporters to take the SIM cards out of their smartphones, stop using bank cards, relocate without disclosing their new addresses to anybody, minimize communication, and, if necessary, communicate only via Telegram. If messages asking "How are you?" or "Where are you?" appear, one should reply that they have already left Kyiv, Nezalezhko advised, telling his viewers that he had received such messages after about 20 of his friends were imprisoned (2022a, 2:45–52:58). Finally, he suggested his followers find ways to leave Ukraine "because this gestapo is trying to find some new and simplified means of identification" (Nezalezhko, 2022a, 5:18–25:24) not only to detain oppositionists but also to send them to the front lines of the war.

Nezalezhko (2022a) laid responsibility for the conflict on Zelensky and "his entourage," who "did everything possible so that the Anglo-Saxons could arrange this war" (16:47–16:57). After leaving Ukraine, Nezalezhko—together with other political immigrants from Ukraine—established the online bilingual (Russian-Ukrainian) channel Mriya (Мрія) focusing on Ukraine's contemporary affairs (www.youtube.com/@mriya). Clearly, this channel is very critical of Zelensky's politics. All the nodal points of the oppositional discourse analyzed in this book are actively discussed in its programs: the Maidan coup d'état, the civil war in Donbas, external control, the prosecution of dissent, and so forth.

However, as in the cases of Montyan and Sharij, Nezalezhhko's criticism of post-Maidan Ukraine has not safeguarded him from attacks by the Russian propaganda machine, of which he is also critical. As just one example, when many political immigrants from Ukraine (Montyan, 2022c) were outraged by the negotiated release of the well-known Ukrainian paramedic Yulia Payevskaya with the call sign "Tayra," who served in the Azov battalion[5] and appeared in Russian media as a perpetrator of atrocities, Nezalezhko addressed those responsible for Russia's information policy. "I would like to understand," he inquired:

What the hell is going on? On federal [TV] channels, you are saying that, covering herself with children, she [Tayra] tried to leave Mariupol after killing the parents of these children. Now, you release her. Are you freaking out there? . . . This happens while Mikhail and Alexander Kononovich [Ukrainian oppositionists] are still in the dungeons of the SSU. Yan Taxiur, Dmitry Marunich, Yuri Tkachev and many, MANY OTHERS, are in [Ukrainian] prisons. . . . How do you, without resolving their issue, release the Maidan panhead that took part in the hostilities? If your task was to anger the pro-Russian asset and raise the spirits of Saloreikh, [6] then the goal has been achieved!

(Nezalezhko, 2022b)

Russian propagandists responded to this and similar posts by Ukrainian political immigrants by harshly attacking them and calling them "slime, carrion [жижа и падаль] and traitors working for the SSU and British intelligence" (Montyan, 2022a, 2022b). Their main lines of argument were that, first, no bloggers had a right to criticize the decisions of the Russian authorities; second, by criticizing Russia, Ukrainian bloggers were serving the interests of Russia's enemies; and third, Russia should not bother itself with efforts to free Ukrainian dissidents—it should instead focus on securing the release of its own captured soldiers (Nezalezhko, 2022c, 13:35–13:51). Painfully reminiscent of what Zhirinovsky told Buzina in 2015 (see Chapter 4), this example is just another illustration of the obvious fact that Ukrainian "others," prosecuted in Ukraine for their political views, are not necessarily welcome in Russia, of which they are often critical as well.

The Repression of Dissent

Addressing his transnational community of "civilized people," Zelensky has repeatedly argued that, "today, the most important thing is to win the information war. This is a war of truth that comes from journalism. . . . Do not spread disinformation, which is carried by the narrative of the Russian Federation. Tell the truth" (Zelensky, 2022g, 7:34–38:03). As it is clear from this message, "truthful" narratives, in Zelensky's sense, cannot overlap with Russian ones; any narratives that do are inherently false. "The world has no right to listen to Russia's false narratives," he told CBS (Zelensky, 2022h). While speaking to the participants of the Shangri-La Dialogue security summit, Zelensky explained that Russia's "disinformation thesis" is that its war against Ukraine "is allegedly something about NATO, about the role of America, about the West's attempts to advance somewhere in Europe" (Zelensky, 2022d, 5:52–56:08). In other words, anybody who would dare to link the ongoing war with NATO expansion and the interests of the military-industrial complex of the United States would be considered a mouthpiece for Russia.

This happened to the British musician Roger Waters of Pink Floyd fame, after a CNN interview in which he criticized the role of the U.S. government in the Russia–Ukraine war and argued that the conflict hinged on "the action and reaction of NATO pushing right up to the Russian border" (Project Censored, 2022). Waters was immediately declared an "enemy of Ukraine" and his name was put on *Myrotvorets*. The same destiny awaited numerous other well-known foreign public figures who dared to articulate the conflict not in the way considered "true" by the government of Ukraine. Among them are Oliver Stone, Henry Kissinger, John Mearsheimer, and many others, including hundreds of foreign journalists who have visited Donbas (IMI, 2016).

"An information attack today is no weaker than a missile attack," Zelensky maintained while communicating with journalists from Poland (Zelensky, 2022b, 6:47–56:54). "It is very important that the information weapon is aimed not at one's own head, but against the enemy," he argued while speaking to Ukrainian journalists (Zelensky, 2022c, 2:55–63:03). "I respect the profession of a journalist. And I distinguish [true journalists] from fake journalists who carry lies"—this is what Zelensky told journalists from Denmark (Zelensky, 2022e, 51:15–51:21). "I am not fighting any journalists. Thank God we have freedom of speech in Ukraine. They have the right to write and think what they want," he argued while communicating with the academic community of Israel (Zelensky, 2022f, 24:49–25:00). As should be clear from the stories of oppositional journalists and bloggers discussed in this book, the implication of Zelensky's message is that he does not fight against journalists who "carry the truth"—that is, those who amplify the Ukrainian government's propaganda—while all others with alternative views should not feel protected. However, as suggested by the story of Andrei Wojciechowski, an Honored Journalist of Ukraine residing in Kharkiv, even those who supported the Maidan and who can hardly be considered enemies of the post-Maidan regime may not feel safe in today's Ukraine, either.

Andrei Wojciechowski[7]

Wojciechowski is a well-known Kharkiv journalist who hosted the TV program *I Think So* before it was shut down. The pro-Russia activist Gennady Makarov (disappeared in May 2022) had been a frequent guest on the program and once characterized it as "the most democratic platform for discussing topical socio-political problems in Kharkiv," with speakers representing many different outlooks invited to participate (Smirnov, 2022). However, even though Wojciechowski's program welcomed the expression of both pro-Maidan and anti-Maidan viewpoints, he himself had been well known for his support of both the Orange Revolution of 2004 and the Euromaidan of 2014. Unlike the other journalists and bloggers whose cases are discussed in this book, Wojciechowski could hardly be considered an "enemy of the state/ people" in this sense.

Nonetheless, he was arrested on May 10, 2022, and charged under Article 111 (treason) for alleged contacts with Russian journalists and officers of Russia's Federal Security Service. For two weeks after Wojciechowski's detainment nobody, including his wife, knew where he had gone. In total, Wojciechowski spent about two months in various Kharkiv prison institutions before his release on July 12 following an acquittal in court, possibly secured through his personal connections with Arsen Avakov, a post-Maidan Minister of Internal Affairs (2014–21), and Yury Lutsenko, a post-Maidan Prosecutor General (2016–19) (Smirnov, 2022).

According to Wojciechowski's (2022) account of what happened, on May 10, he left his house for a walk with the dog. A minibus pulled up immediately. Somebody put a pillowcase over his head and wrapped it with adhesive tape; he was then handcuffed from behind, thrown flat into the bus, and taken in an unknown direction. About 20 minutes later, he was taken into a basement, where he was stripped naked and subjected to interrogation. Through later conversations with experts, Wojciechowski learned that the methods used on him were not as brutal as in a so-called "enhanced interrogation": It ended with his teeth and jaws still intact, and he had no marks on his body beyond the traces on his wrists from very tight handcuffs. During the questioning, Wojciechowski was asked what connections he had with Russian journalists, if he was an agent of the Kremlin, and so forth. "Compared to other people, they treated me gently," he claimed (Wojciechowski, 2022, 1:28–32:53).

So how were other political prisoners treated? Wojciechowski's account is terrifying. At first, he was alone in the cell, but then he was locked up with the mayor of Stary Saltov—a city of the Kharkiv region, which was a site of fierce battles between Russian and Ukrainian troops in the spring of 2022—who was charged under Article 111, part 2, and facing up to life imprisonment. On the third or fourth day, a prisoner from Zolochev—another city in the Kharkiv oblast—was brought into the cell; his head was tightly wrapped with tape. He was breathing heavily and complained all the time of pain in his lungs and heart. This man died about six hours later, and Wojciechowski took him out of the cell. "His son was also badly beaten with broken ribs, (and) was in a neighboring cell," he explained (Wojciechowski, 2022, 3:50–54:52). The other cell held about 15 people in a space so small they had to take turns sleeping on the floor.

Wojciechowski also described the stories of other political prisoners with whom he communicated during bus rides to interrogation sessions. He observed that most people brought in under Article 111 were arrested for very minor or even innocuous things: congratulating people on May 9[8] on social networks or describing the situation in Kharkiv for friends and relatives in Russia, for example. "In fact, frivolous statements," he asserted. Other young people were taken in for filming for themselves how "Grads"—multiple rocket launchers—worked. As Wojciechowski says, they "were severely beaten up: broken ribs, damaged lungs, hands twisted with wire, and the like."

They were required to admit that they had been sending this video footage to Russian intelligence or Russian agents (Wojciechowski, 2022, 10:00–11:29).

After two months in prison, Wojciechowski was released; he did not receive any criminal punishment, but he "cannot rejoice," as he put it. For him, it was very sad that Putin attacked Ukraine, and pitiful that Kharkiv was crumbling and Kharkovites dying. But even amid hostilities, he argued, people should live more peacefully and not provoke conflicts over opposing viewpoints. He explained,

> I have a neighbor who says: "During the war there should not be two or three points of view. . . . " Should we really all unite and be as one in certain matters? But what if humanitarian aid is being stolen, if weapons are being stolen, something else is being done: attacks on the Russian language, terrible statements, and so on and so forth? There should not be one opinion on these matters.
>
> (2022, 12:54–13:49)

As highlighted earlier, Wojciechowski is not an "anti-Maidan other"; even his account of his imprisonment can hardly be regarded as oppositional in the sense that, unlike other journalists/bloggers whose discursive constructions are analyzed in this book, he does not link the current war with the Maidan, the Donbas "anti-terrorist operation," external control, or other nodal points of the oppositional discourse. However, like other oppositional journalists and bloggers, he also emphasized the links between the current Ukrainian government and blatant violations of human rights and freedoms, including the civil rights of Russian speakers. Moreover, he openly challenged Zelensky's populist claim regarding the unity of all Ukrainians in their opinions regarding the war.

Importantly, as Wojciechowski's articulation suggests, the necessity of defending a uniform vision of what is going on in the war has been propagated by those Ukrainian officials trying to avoid public scrutiny over the looting of humanitarian aid and weapons, as well as other misconduct. One recent example of this trend is a criminal case opened with respect to the publication by *Ukrainska Pravda*—a popular Ukrainian news site—of a report on Kyrylo Tymoshenko, the Deputy Head of the President's Office. According to the publication, amid the current war, when millions of people are deprived of basic necessities, Tymoshenko is driving a 2021 Porsche Taycan worth about US$100,000. Following the publication of the report, the Serious Crimes Investigation Team of the Investigations Division of the Main Directorate of the National Police of Kyiv started "a criminal investigation into allegations of the unauthorized copying of information from the Safe City video surveillance camera system" (*Ukrainska Pravda*, 2022). This story is a good illustration of Wojciechowski's point regarding a "unified opinion" serving as a convenient cover for those in power who use wartime as an opportunity for personal enrichment.

Conclusion

In this chapter, I have considered three cases of Ukrainian journalists and bloggers whose stories help destabilize further the dichotomization of the social prescribed by Zelensky's populist discourse. Connecting the post-Maidan government of Ukraine predominantly with violations of human rights and freedoms, all three figures, despite their differences, share one key similarity. They all make clear that the ostensible unity of Ukraine fighting against a tyrannical Russia has been achieved by means of arresting, torturing, prosecuting, and killing those who hold alternative views. Obviously, this has nothing to do with Zelensky's claim that Ukraine is defending democracy against tyranny, but it has a lot to do with what George Orwell (1945) observed back in the middle of the last century: "There is now a widespread tendency to argue that one can only defend democracy by totalitarian methods. If one loves democracy, the argument runs, one must crush its enemies by no matter what means. . . . In other words, defending democracy involves destroying all independence of thought." This is exactly what we observe in Ukraine, and it is very unlikely that this totalitarian closure—achieved by both discursive and nondiscursive means—will serve to defend democracy, as Zelensky wants the whole world to believe.

While I finished writing this chapter, another piece of news arrived. On December 29, 2022, over the objections of media unions and press freedom organizations that warned the move would have a chilling effect on free speech (Patil, 2022), Zelensky signed into law an expansion of the government's regulatory power in the media sphere (Dress, 2023). The law, which, in the opinion of the European Federation of Journalists, "is worthy of the worst authoritarian regimes" (Kiev Independent, 2022), ramps up the powers of the media regulator, known as National Security on Radio and TV, by granting it the authority to shut down news sites and fine them without a court ruling (Law on Media, 2022). Through this law, the entire information space of Ukraine is being taken under strict control. Without a VPN, even social networks can no longer provide Ukrainians with alternative information, given that platforms such as YouTube and Facebook have allowed oppositional channels to be blocked. The only exception seems to be Telegram, which is currently beyond the control of Ukrainian regulators.

Notes

1 I had a chance to communicate with Tkachev personally in 2019 while researching the Odessa tragedy; prior to that, I had been following his publications on a regular basis.
2 Vladimir Struk was abducted and killed in March 2022. His killing has been reported as a response to his pro-Russian stance.
3 The Immortal Regiment [Бессмертный полк] is a massive civil event held in Russia on May 9 during the Victory Day celebrations. Participants carry the pictures of relatives who struggled against fascism in the Great Patriotic War (1941–45).

4 Nezalezhko's YouTube channel was blocked in January 2023.
5 Established in May 2014 as a volunteer paramilitary militia to fight in the Donbas war, the Azov regiment is widely known for its association with Nazi ideology and the use of Nazi symbols, as well as for allegations of war crimes (Grayzone, n/d).
6 This neologism created from two words—salo (pork fat, a national Ukrainian dish) and Reich—is used by Ukrainian oppositional bloggers to denote Ukraine's totalitarian tendency to prosecute dissidents.
7 I have known Wojciechowski personally since 1991, when I started working as a TV news reporter at ATN, a local news production company.
8 May 9 is the Victory Day over fascism in the Great Patriotic War; its celebration is now forbidden in Ukraine, in line with the policy of "decommunization." What is allowed instead is commemoration of the victims of the Second World War, with no Soviet or Communist symbols permitted.

Reference List

Baysha, O. (2020a). Dehumanizing political others: A discursive-material perspective. *Critical Discourse Studies*, *17*(3), 292–307. doi:10.1080/17405904.2019.1567364

Baysha, O. (2020b). The antagonistic discourses of the Euromaidan: Koloradi, sovki, and vatniki vs. jumpers, maidowns, and panheads. In N. Knoblock (Ed.), *Language of conflict: Discourses of the Ukrainian crisis* (pp. 101–117). Bloomsbury Academic.

Baysha, O. (2020c). The dangerous Russian other in Ukrainian conspiratorial discourse: Media representations of the Odessa tragedy. In A. Astapova, O. Colăcel, C. Pintilescu, & T. Scheibner (Eds.), *Conspiracy theories in Eastern Europe* (pp. 167–185). Routledge.

Censor. (2014a, May 3). *Odessa tragedy is part of Russia's plan to split Ukraine* (in Russian). https://censor.net.ua/news/283775/tradiya_v_odesse_eto_chast_plana_rossii_po_raskolu_ukrainy_poroshenko

Censor. (2014b, May 3). *Tymoshenko arrived in Odessa* (in Russian). https://censor.net.ua/news/283697/timoshenko_pribyla_v_odessu

Council of Europe. (2015, November 4). Report of the international advisory panel. *Council of Europe*. https://rm.coe.int/CoERMPublicCommonSearchServices/DisplayDCTMContent?documentId=090000168048610f

Dress, B. (2023, January 1). Zelensky signs controversial law expanding government power to regulate media. *Hill*. https://thehill.com/homenews/3795160-zelensky-signs-controversial-law-expanding-government-power-to-regulate-media

EuroMaydan. (2014, May 2). Kolorado tents on the Kulikovo Field are almost gone (in Ukrainian). *Facebook*. www.facebook.com/search/top/?q=%D0%84%D0%B2%D1%80%D0%BE%D0%9C%D0%B0%D0%B9%D0%B4%D0%B0%D0%BD%20%E2%80%93%20EuroMaydan%20%D0%BA%D0%BE%D0%BB%D0%BE%D1%80%D0%B0%D0%B4%D1%81%D1%8C%D0%BA%D0%B8%D1%85%20%D0%BD%D0%B0%D0%BC%D0%B5%D1%82%D1%96%D0%B2&epa=SEARCH_BOX

Gordon. (2014, May 3). *Tymoshenko arrived in Odessa* (in Russian). https://gordonua.com/news/separatism/timoshenko-priehala-v-odessu-20880.html

Grayzone. (n/d). *Azov Battalion*. https://thegrayzone.com/tag/azov-battalion/

ICTV. (2014, May 3). *Tymoshenko: We are able to defend Ukraine* (in Ukrainian). https://fakty.com.ua/ua/videos/60763

IMI. (2016, May 24). "Myrotvorets" published a list of foreign journalists "accredited" in "DPR." *Institute of Mass Information.* https://imi.org.ua/en/news/myrotvorets-published-list-of-foreign-journalists-accredited-in -dpr-i26243

IMI. (2022, March 20). Zelensky put into effect decision on unique telethon "United News #UARAZOM." *Institute of Mass Information.* https://imi.org.ua/en/news/zelensky-put-into-effect-decision-on-unique-telethon-united-news-uarazom-i44486

Kiev Independent. (2022, December 30). *Zelensky signs media law criticized by journalist groups as authoritarian.* https://kyivindependent.com/news-feed/zelensky-signs-media-law-criticized-by-journalist-groups-as-authoritarian

Law on Media. (2022, December 13). *The Law of Ukraine about the media.* https://zakon.rada.gov.ua/laws/show/2849-IX#Text

Montyan, T. (2022a, June 21). Drooling splashes in all directions (in Russian). *Telegram.* https://t.me/montyan2/1628

Montyan, T. (2022b, June 22). Seryoga, Seryoga . . . (in Russian). *Telegram.* https://t.me/montyan2/1647

Montyan, T. (2022c, June 30). It's not about the exchange! (in Russian). *Telegram.* https://t.me/montyan2/1764

Nezalezhko, T. (2015, July 30). Jump, bitch! (in Russian). *YouTube.* www.youtube.com/watch?v=OtaBUg-IpmM

Nezalezhko, T. (2022a, April 12). How to survive and flee Ukraine (in Russian). *YouTube.* www.youtube.com/watch?v=47anv9aOPaw

Nezalezhko, T. (2022b, June 18). I would like to understand. . . . (in Russian). *Telegram.* https://t.me/tarik_nezalejko/4399

Nezalezhko, T. (2022c, June 20). From Politvera to Tayra is one step (in Russian). *YouTube.* www.youtube.com/watch?v=Wn7MhfkGgkM

Orwell, G. (1945). The freedom of the press. *The Orwell Foundation.* www.orwellfoundation.com/the-orwell-foundation/orwell/essays-and-other-works/the-freedom-of-the-press

Patil, A. (2022, December 30). Critics say a new media law signed by Zelensky could restrict press freedom in Ukraine. *New York Times.* www.nytimes.com/2022/12/30/world/europe/zelensky-journalism-law-free-speech.html

Project Censored. (2022, December 1). *Roger Waters declared "enemy of Ukraine" on Myrotvorets Website.* www.projectcensored.org/roger-waters-declared-enemy-of-ukraine-on-myrotvorets-website/

Segodnya. (2014a, May 3). *The tragedy in Odessa occurred due to an external provocation* (in Russian). www.segodnya.ua/regions/odessa/tragediya-v-odesse-proizoshla-iz-za-vneshney-provokacii-turchinov-517522.html

Segodnya. (2014b, May 3). *Most of the participants in Odessa riots are the citizens of Russia and Transdnistria* (in Russian). www.segodnya.ua/hot/odessa-pozhar-stolkn/bolshinstvo-uchastnikov-besporyadkov-v-odesse-grazhdane-rossii-i-pridnestrovy-amiliciya-517552.html

Sharij, A. (2022, June 9). Tkachev is released on bail (in Russian). *Telegram.* https://t.me/ASupersharij/9673

Smirnov, I. (2022, August 1). Fully justified: A scandalous Kharkiv journalist left the pre-trial detention center (In Russian). *Politnavigator.* www.politnavigator.net/polnostyu-opravdan-iz-sizo-vyshel-skandalnyjj-kharkovskijj-zhurnalist.html

Tkachev, Y. (2022a, February 23). I am asked . . . (in Russian). *Telegram.* https://t.me/dadzibao/5466

Tkachev, Y. (2022b, February 24). Vladimir Alexandrovich . . . (in Russian). *Telegram.* https://t.me/dadzibao/5482

Tkachev, Y. (2022c, February 24). We do understand, don't we? (in Russian). *Telegram.* https://t.me/dadzibao/5534

Tkachev, Y. (2022d, February 24). To be honest, there is no time for reflections (in Russian). *Telegram.* https://t.me/dadzibao/5557

Tkachev, Y. (2022e, February 25). Apart from the military situation . . . (in Russian). *Telegram.* https://t.me/dadzibao/5624

Tkachev, Y. (2022f, March 3). The monstrous aftermath of an airstrike (in Russian). *Telegram.* https://t.me/dadzibao/6069

Tkachev, Y. (2022g, March 8). I think you have already seen the SSU video (in Russian). *Telegram.* https://t.me/dadzibao/6454

Tkachev, Y. (2022h, March 12). Zelensky: The kidnapping of the mayor of Melitopol. . . . (in Russian). *Telegram.* https://t.me/dadzibao/6632

Tkachev, Y. (2022i, March 12). On Ukraine and Nazi (in Russian). *Telegram.* https://t.me/dadzibao/6637

Tkachev, Y. (2022j, March 18). The SSU continues to terrorize the unreliable (in Russian). *Telegram.* https://t.me/dadzibao/7052

TSN. (2014, May 3). Bloody clashes in Odessa took the lives of 43 people (in Ukrainian). *1 + 1.* https://tsn.ua/ukrayina/krivavi-sutichki-vodesi-zabrali-zhittya-43-osib-25-perebuvayut-u-tyazhkomu-stani-347951.html

Ukrainska Pravda. (2022, December 3). *Police look for those who helped Ukrainska Pravda identify deputy head of the President's office in an expensive car.* www.pravda.com.ua/eng/news/2022/12/3/7379125/

UN OHCHR. (2014, June 15). *Report on the human rights situation in Ukraine.* Office of the United Nations High Commissioner for Human Rights. www.ohchr.org/Documents/Countries/UA/HRMMUReport15June2014.pdf.

Wilayto, P. (2022, March 29). Political repression in Ukraine. *Popular Resistance.* https://popularresistance.org/political-repression-in-ukraine

Wojciechowski, A. (2022, July 22). *Why was Wojciechowski imprisoned?* (in Russian). *YouTube.* www.youtube.com/watch?v=Umm7kbJIKmA

Yasinsky, O. (2022, March 21). Witchhunt in Ukraine against journalists, activists and left-wing politicians. *Pressenza.* www.pressenza.com/2022/03/witchhunt-in-ukraine-against-journalists-activists-and-left-wing-politicians/?fbclid=IwAR2Q6V5qxNBFmwd1OQm-NLj1UxJyxxwNSMyKn9pqE7xkDDHhQ9DRJbubeN8&mibextid=ATveJy

Zelensky, V. (2021, February 5). Volodymyr Zelensky first recorded his appeal in Russian for the first time (in Russian). *YouTube.* www.youtube.com/watch?v=yw8lNQ4hlj4

Zelensky, V. (2022a, March 20). An evening address of the President of Ukraine Volodymyr Zelensky to Ukrainians (in Ukrainian). *YouTube.* www.youtube.com/watch?v=LFi62XVLJSE

Zelensky, V. (2022b, April 29). Volodymyr Zelensky spoke with representatives of the Polish mass media (in Ukrainian). *YouTube.* www.youtube.com/watch?v=uobFhTgr96k

Zelensky, V. (2022c, June 6). Volodymyr Zelensky's conversation with media representatives on journalist's day (in Ukrainian). *YouTube.* www.youtube.com/watch?v=yrNA01enl04

Zelensky, V. (2022d, June 11). Zelensky addressed the participants of the Shangri-La Dialogue Asian security summit (in Ukrainian). *YouTube*. www.youtube.com/watch?v=0QcS-ptla9A

Zelensky, V. (2022e, June 14). Zelensky gave an online press conference for representatives of the Danish media (in Ukrainian). *YouTube*. www.youtube.com/watch?v=7e0X_FQPpXo

Zelensky, V. (2022f, June 23). Zelensky talked with students and professors of Israel (in Ukrainian). *YouTube*. www.youtube.com/watch?v=Inu_d1uXj3E&t=2s

Zelensky, V. (2022g, August 4). Zelensky spoke with media representatives from Nigeria, South Africa, Kenya and Ghana (in Ukrainian). *YouTube*. www.youtube.com/watch?v=XmDAunwxtec

Zelensky, V. (2022h, September 25). The full transcript of an interview with Ukrainian President Volodymyr Zelensky … on "face the nation." *CBS*. www.cbsnews.com/news/volodymyr-zelenskyy-ukraine-president-face-the-nation-transcript-09-25-2022/

6   The Deadlock of the Peace Treaty

Ilovaisk and Debaltseve Battles

Since the beginning of the Donbas war in the spring of 2014, numerous efforts have been made to establish a ceasefire and proceed toward a political solution acceptable for both sides—Donbas rebels supported by Russia (the self-proclaimed Donetsk People's Republic, DPR, and the Luhansk People's Republic, LPR) and the Ukrainian government. The first diplomatic attempt to achieve a compromise was made in April 2014. This quadrilateral "Geneva format" initiative, with Ukraine, Russia, the EU, and the United States attempting to resolve the issue through negotiation, failed to make headway. The second format of negotiations was the Trilateral Contact Group on Ukraine, consisting of representatives from Ukraine, Russia, and the Organization for Security and Cooperation in Europe (OSCE). It is within this format that the Minsk I treaty was prepared and signed by Ukraine, Russia, and representatives of the DPR and LPR on September 5, 2014 (Kostanyan & Meister, 2016). This agreement became possible after the decisive rout of the Ukrainian Army in the battle of Ilovaisk (August 7–September 2, 2014).

Ilovaisk

Ilovaisk is a small town in the Donetsk region, 40 kilometers south of the city of Donetsk. Since May 2014, it has been controlled by armed groups of the self-proclaimed DPR. In early August 2014, Ukrainian armed forces launched an operation to regain control of the city. By this time, much of the area held by Donbas fighters had already been recaptured by the Ukrainian army and Ukrainian volunteer battalions, the channels of communication between the Donetsk and Luhansk republics had been disrupted, and the defeat of the uprising looked imminent (Cohen & Green, 2016).

Ukrainian armed units entered Ilovaisk on August 19; the largest part of the city was very soon under Ukraine's control, and the undeclared war, which was called an "anti-terrorist operation," seemed to be almost over. The next day, however, the fighting unexpectedly intensified. To the surprise of the Ukrainian

DOI: 10.4324/9781003379164-9

military, victory in the effort was no longer assured. On August 24, Ukrainian media reported that Ilovaisk was surrounded by Russian troops (Shramovych, 2019). Many believe the encirclement happened due to the intervention of Russian regular military units that had crossed the border shortly before the Ilovaisk battle to provide help for Donbas fighters, although the Kremlin has always denied that the regular Russian army participated in the Donbas war. According to Putin, the reinforcements there were only volunteers who "at the call of the heart fulfill their duty" (Interfax-Ukraine, 2014).

On August 28, information appeared that negotiations were taking place, and that a "green corridor" for Ukrainian soldiers was being prepared (Shramovych, 2019). Late at night, Putin called on the Donbas fighters "to open a humanitarian corridor for Ukrainian servicemen who were surrounded in order to avoid senseless victims" (Putin, 2014). This information was posted on the Kremlin's official website at around 1 p.m. on August 29, 2014. Earlier that same day, Ukrainian military forces received the command to gather and withdraw from Ilovaisk in two columns, but those leaving through the evacuation corridor soon found themselves under fire.

In the Ukrainian account of events, this was a vile breach of the agreement. Meanwhile, the pro-Russian side maintained that Ukrainian troops were allowed to use the corridor and leave the "cauldron" under the condition that no weapons could be taken from the field. Despite this, according to the pro-Russian side's account, Ukrainian military units were ordered to break through the corridor in a fighting retreat, and this is why their columns "were met by artillery fire" (Apukhtin, 2020). Whichever version is correct, far from all the encircled Ukrainian troops were able to escape from the Ilovaisk "cauldron." According to Ukrainian officials, 366 of them were killed. The estimate of Ukraine's death toll provided by the Russian side is much higher—more than 1,000 lives (Apukhtin, 2020).

In Russia and Donbas, many people expected that Ilovaisk was just the beginning of a larger military campaign that would lead to the complete defeat of the Ukrainian army. This did not happen, however; Russian leadership used the defeat of the Ukrainian army near Ilovaisk to force the Ukrainian leadership to sit down at the negotiating table. Many anti-Maidan Ukrainians were shocked by this outcome. They could not believe that Russia would stop halfway and leave Donbas under Kyiv's rule (e.g., Melnikov, 2022). However, after the collapse of the Ilovaisk "cauldron," Minsk I was signed on September 5, providing for the return of Donbas to Ukraine, albeit with a special status (Protocol, 2014).

Minsk I never worked out, however; it completely fell apart at the beginning of 2015, when the armed forces of the DPR and LPR launched a new offensive. On January 21, they were able to achieve a significant symbolic victory by capturing Donetsk International Airport, the last part of the city of Donetsk that had been under the control of Ukrainian armed forces. Inspired by the feat, the armies of the self-proclaimed republics developed their offensive further, setting their sights on the important railway and road junctions of Debaltseve city.

Debaltseve

The battle of Debaltseve was the last major battle of the Donbas war and led to the Minsk II ceasefire agreement. Debaltseve came under the control of Donbas insurgents in April 2014. On July 28, 2014, Ukrainian armed forces managed to recapture the city; it was then under Ukraine's control until late January 2015, when DPR forces attacked the Ukrainian positions (Tucker, 2015a).

On January 28, 2015, DPR fighters captured the highway leading into Debaltseve, which allowed them to encircle most of the city. The next day, they took control of Vuhlehisk, a town to the west of Debaltseve, which made the situation even more difficult for Ukrainian troops. According to Russian sources, about 8,000 Ukrainian troops were encircled at that moment (Zinets & Dyomkin, 2015). By the beginning of February, the expression "Debaltseve cauldron" came to be widely used (Kramer, 2015). Despite serious reinforcements coming to assist the Ukrainian troops, the Debaltseve cauldron was completely "closed" on February 9 (Tucker, 2015b). The situation was reminiscent of Ilovaisk, though with a larger scale of defeat and likely much heavier losses. Estimates of the number of Ukrainian troops killed ranged from 250 to as many as 3,000. Hundreds of Ukrainian soldiers were captured.

The military escalation prompted another cycle of negotiations. This time they took place within the context of the so-called "Normandy format," which involved Ukraine, Russia, Germany, and France. French President François Hollande and German Chancellor Angela Merkel put forth a new peace plan, which was a revival of the first Minsk agreement (BBC, 2015). On February 11, in Minsk, the capital of Belarus, a summit took place in which Russian president Vladimir Putin, Ukrainian president Petro Poroshenko, DPR leader Alexander Zakharchenko, and LPR leader Igor Plotnitsky along with Hollande and Merkel negotiated on the Franco-German diplomatic plan (Soldatkin & Polityuk, 2015). On February 12, 2015, it was announced that the parties had agreed on the Package of Measures for the Implementation of the Minsk Agreements, widely referred to as Minsk II (OSCE, 2015).

No Talks With "Terrorists"

The terms of Minsk II were substantially worse for Kyiv than the terms of the unfulfilled Minsk I. The harshest part of the agreement was its political prescriptions such as decentralizing power in Ukraine through amending the Constitution, adopting a law on the special status of ORDLO ("temporarily occupied territories of Ukraine") and holding elections in these regions according to a new law. Some key passages read as follows (emphasis added):

4. *On the first day after the withdrawal* [of troops], to begin a dialogue on the procedures for holding *local elections* in accordance with Ukrainian law and the Law of Ukraine "On a temporary order of local government in individual areas of the Donetsk and Luhansk regions . . ."

9. *Restoration of full control over the state border of Ukraine* by Ukraine's government throughout the whole conflict area, which should begin *on the first day after the local elections* and be completed after a comprehensive political settlement (local elections in individual areas of the Donetsk and Luhansk regions on the basis of the Law of Ukraine, and a constitutional reform) by the end of 2015, on condition of implementation of paragraph 11—with consultations and in agreement with *the representatives of individual areas of the Donetsk and Luhansk regions* in the framework of the Trilateral Contact Group.

11. Conducting *constitutional reform in Ukraine*, with the new constitution coming into force by the end of 2015, providing for *decentralization* as a key element (taking into account the characteristics of individual areas of the Donetsk and Luhansk regions, *agreed with representatives of these areas*), as well as the adoption of the permanent legislation on the *special status of individual areas of the Donetsk and Luhansk regions* in accordance with the measures specified in Note [1], until the end of 2015.

(UNIAN, 2015, emphasis added)

The creation of wide autonomy for Donbas within decentralization—a "special status"—would have made it effectively impossible for Ukraine to join Western institutions such as NATO and the EU because such autonomy "would potentially give it [Donbas] veto power over national goals such as NATO and EU membership" (Nardelli, 2021). This idea from Russia was hardly acceptable for the post-Maidan political establishment of Ukraine with its agenda of Euro-Atlantic integration, in the name of which the Euromaidan had been initiated. However, as is evident from the ninth paragraph of the agreement, Ukraine's border control in the region would only be restored if the constitutional reform and decentralization requirements were fulfilled (Allan, 2020).

After the defeat in Debaltseve, President Poroshenko had no choice but to sign Minsk II to avoid greater losses; he also wanted to use the ceasefire as a respite to accumulate strength. As he acknowledged in June 2022, the task was "to knock out eight years to restore economic growth and build the strength of the armed forces" (Poroshenko, 2022). Later, this was confirmed by German ex-Chancellor Angela Merkel and ex-President of France François Hollande. In an interview with *Die Zeit* in December 2022, Merkel said, "The 2014 Minsk Agreement was an attempt to buy time for Ukraine. Ukraine used this time to become stronger, as you can see today." According to Merkel, "it was clear for everyone" that the conflict was suspended and the problem was not resolved, "but it was exactly what gave Ukraine the priceless time" (Newsroom, 2022). "Angela Merkel is right on this point," Hollande echoed in an interview for the *Kyiv Independent* later the same month. "Since 2014, Ukraine has strengthened its military posture. . . . It is the merit of the Minsk agreements to have given the Ukrainian army this opportunity" (Prouvost, 2022). In other words, despite the signed agreement, Kyiv—backed by its Western partners—had no intention to fulfill the terms of Minsk II and grant autonomy to the rebellious region. In February 2023, Zelensky admitted that he was also unwilling to implement the Minsk agreements (Roshchina, 2023).

Although the trick became public knowledge only in 2022, after it was acknowledged by Poroshenko, Merkel, and Hollande, many oppositionists understood the situation much earlier. As Montyan put it while speaking to the UN on February 19, 2022:

> I am absolutely sure that you all know very well that the Kyiv authorities never intended to fulfill the Minsk agreements. . . . For them it was just a break in order to say "yes, we will fulfill [the agreements], and during this time the West will pump us with weapons and strengthen our armed forces, and we hope that after some time we will try to recapture the rebellious republics by force."

"It seems, what is the problem with giving a special status?" Montyan went on. "But they [those in power] will not do this because they suppress absolutely any dissent in Ukraine":

> People who are against the Maidan coup d'état and against the [Donbas] war . . . do not have any right to speak anywhere at all. They have no political parties and public organizations, they are deprived of the right to vote. . . . [1] And you want the Kyiv regime to negotiate with Luhansk and Donetsk? I am sure that you understand that this will never happen. Never . . . I am sure that the West allows the Kiev regime not to fulfill the Minsk agreements, and if this were not so, all these Minsk agreements would have been fulfilled a long time ago.
>
> (Montyan, 2022a)

Now, after Poroshenko, Merkel, Hollande, and Zelensky have publicly confirmed what Montyan and other oppositionists claimed much earlier, the entire saga of Ukraine's non-implementation of Minsk II can be read as a story of Kyiv maneuvering to avoid fulfilling the agreement.

Minsk II provided specific time spans for implementing many of the agreed-upon measures, but the deadlines turned out to be impossible to meet.

In October 2015, German Foreign Minister and OSCE Chairperson-in-Office Frank-Walter Steinmeier suggested another plan that came to be known as the "Steinmeier Formula"—a simplified version of Minsk II consisting of three consecutive steps. First, elections in ORDLO, observed and validated by the OSCE's Office for Democratic Institutions and Human Rights (ODIHR); second, the entry into force of a new Ukrainian law on a special autonomous status for the regions; and third, the restoration of Ukraine's control over its border with Russia.

President Poroshenko, who had already signed two Minsk agreements, avoided signing the Steinmeier Formula, arguing it was unacceptable to negotiate with "terrorists" (Poroshenko, 2015). This was despite the fact that Poroshenko's signature under the Minsk agreements was adjacent to the signatures of the leaders of the DPR and LPR, with the agreed-upon terms containing a provision about the necessity of consulting with "the representatives of individual areas of the Donetsk and Luhansk regions" (UNIAN, 2015). In contrast to Poroshenko, Zelensky agreed to Steinmeier's formula. On December 9, 2019, at the Normandy forum in Paris, he put his signature under a two-page Declaration in which all the participants—the President of the French Republic, the Chancellor of the Federal Republic of Germany, the President of the Russian Federation, and the President of Ukraine—reconfirmed their commitment to the Minsk agreements and adopted the Steinmeier Formula.

On December 10, 2019, the official site of Ukraine's President Zelensky informed Ukrainians that

The Minsk agreements (Minsk Protocol of September 5, 2014, Minsk Memorandum of September 19, 2014 and Minsk Set of Measures of February 12, 2015) continue to serve as the basis of the Normandy format, the Member States of which are committed to their full implementation.

(President of Ukraine, 2019)

Regarding "measures to implement the political provisions of the Minsk agreements," it was confirmed that

The parties express their interest in reaching agreements within the Normandy format (H4) and the Trilateral Contact Group on all legal aspects of the special order of local self-government (special status) of certain districts of the Donetsk and Luhansk regions—as specified in the Set of Measures for the Implementation of the Minsk agreements of 2015—to ensure its continued operation.

They consider it necessary to incorporate the "Steinmeier formula" into Ukrainian law according to the version agreed by H4 and the Trilateral Contact Group.

(President of Ukraine, 2019)

The presidential site also stated that the participants of the Paris meeting "agreed to hold another meeting in this format within four months as regards political and security conditions, inter alia, to organize local elections" (President of Ukraine, 2019). This meeting never took place.

As is clear from my analysis of Zelensky's speeches following the onset of full-scale war in 2022, he placed the blame for breaking the peace process exclusively on Russia, which he presented as "an insatiable alligator" (Zelensky, 2022e, 24:14–24:21) that "does not want peace" (Zelensky, 2022d, 26:57–27:01). "They say 'we agree,' then they break," Zelensky claimed (Zelensky, 2022b, 17:01–17:05). Despite that Poroshenko, Merkel, and Hollande already affirmed that Minsk II was used by Ukraine to buy time and strengthen its armed forces, Zelensky insisted that the Minsk agreement was intended "to give Russia a rest before the next invasion" (Zelensky, 2022f, 5:14–15:20).

On May 13, 2022, answering the question of why Ukraine was so reluctant to grant Donbas a wide autonomy, Zelensky responded: "They [Russia] recognized [the republics] as separate. . . . They did not discuss the issue of this or that autonomy. No, not like that. They just went to get it" (Zelensky, 2022c, 36:36–38:15). The obvious problem with this statement is that before February 24, 2022, Russia had been insisting on the autonomy of Donbas as part of Ukraine, which was prescribed by the Minsk agreements—it was non-implementation of the agreements by Ukraine that prompted Russia to recognize the DPR and LPR as separate states. Zelensky also tried to assure his audiences that "there is no proof" Ukrainian troops had been shelling Donbas cities since the declaration of the ATO. "Sometimes they are so cynical that they shot themselves," Zelensky claimed (Zelensky, 2022a, 30:27–30:32), repeating a popular meme among pro-Maidan Ukrainians with respect to Donbas people.

In contrast to Zelensky's articulation of the Donbas war and the Minsk agreements, whose non-implementation he ties exclusively to Russia's inherent aggressiveness and hostility, oppositional voices have been linking the Minsk deadlock not only to the geopolitical games of the West but also to Ukrainian ultra-nationalists who protest any potential compromise with the pro-Russian population in the southeast of Ukraine. To make sense of this aspect of the oppositional interpretation, one needs to know that on the eve of his Paris trip, Zelensky met with fierce resistance from nationalists led by Poroshenko. The nationalistic stance was crystal clear: Even the smallest concession to Russia's demands would amount to surrender, regardless of whether these demands were part of an internationally recognized agreement. Right after Zelensky announced his decision to sign the document, thousands of protesters "took to the cobblestone streets of Kyiv and chanted 'No to capitulation' . . . arguing that the formula violates Ukraine's sovereignty" (Lynch, 2019).

Under pressure from nationalists, Zelensky resorted to arguing that Donbas elections would be held only after Russian forces were withdrawn and Ukraine regained control of its border. "There won't be any elections under the barrel of a gun; there won't be any elections there if the troops are still there," Zelensky (BBC, 2019) promised, trying to bat away accusations of conceding to Russia's demands. But the problem with this interpretation was that it contradicted the sequence of events prescribed by the Steinmeier Formula, which Zelensky had already signed.

By making this commitment in a bid to find a peaceful solution, Zelensky had maneuvered himself into a dead end. On the one hand, radicals in the streets and the right-wing parliamentary opposition made it impossible to implement the constitutional reforms prescribed by the Minsk agreements; on the other hand, Russia refused to compromise on the terms of Minsk II, arguing that it was a legal agreement officially adopted by the Organization for Security and Co-operation in Europe (OSCE, 2015) and the Security Council of the United Nations (UN, 2015).

On July 23, 2020—seven months after his signature appeared on the declaration of the Paris summit, which confirmed the commitment of all the parties to the Minsk agreements—Zelensky made the following announcement:

> In the Minsk format, everything should be written out in detail: each person, who answers, when, how this information is transmitted. That is, it will be a separate story, it is very long. We want an interpretation of each point of "Minsk." Then we will see whether we can do it or not, how we will do it, who will be responsible.
>
> (President of Ukraine, 2020)

In Zelensky's numerous speeches at the time, he presented all his attempts to maneuver with the Minsk agreements as efforts to reach peace on "Ukrainian terms." It is unclear why he thought this would work, but there were many alternative voices in Ukraine that warned about the dangers of such a game. Nowadays, these voices are silenced, including Dmitry Dzhangirov, whose point of view on the issue I will briefly present in the following section.

Cutting the Gordian Knot of the Minsk Agreements

Dmitry Dzhangirov[2]

Dzhangirov is a well-known Ukrainian publicist, journalist, and blogger specializing in political analysis. From the first years of Ukrainian independence until his arrest in March 2022, he worked as an editor-in-chief and analyst for media with a national audience; he also managed the Kyiv TV and Radio Company from 2007 to 2010. In recent years, Dzhangirov had primarily been running his YouTube channel, *Capital* (www.youtube.com/c/CapitalUa). Known for his leftist views and criticism of the post-Maidan governments, Dzhangirov, as some sources indicate, was arrested in March 2022 by the SSU along with other critics of the post-Maidan political regime (Myrolub, 2022). No public news about him has been heard since March 8—the day his last video was released (Dzhangirov, 2022c)—making it unclear if Dzhangirov was really arrested by the SSU or if he may have been abducted by radicals. As Montyan (2022b) claimed, the banking code posted on Dzhangirov's You-Tube channel for viewers to contribute funding was changed to a code exactly matching that of Serhii Prytula, a well-known Ukrainian "activist."

For the purposes of this book, I have chosen Dzhangirov's (2020) You-Tube video devoted to the speech in which Zelensky sought an interpretation of each point of the Minsk agreements to understand whether or not they could be implemented (see the previous section). Dzhangirov called it "a weird statement" because "it is very strange to ask to explain what is written now, after more than six months after the Paris meeting" (Dzhangirov, 2020, 8:52–59:20). Dzhangirov reminded his audience that it was common to refer to the commitments signed in Paris as "homework" to be fulfilled before the next meeting could take place. The act of signing the document—the "roadmap," as many also called it—implied that "all the parties understand it equally," including Zelensky, whose signature on the summit's declaration "testifies that he understands it in the same way as others" (Dzhangirov, 2020, 10:35–11:06). Because the Paris declaration was a derivative of the Minsk agreements, Dzhangirov went on, "it is implied that if you sign this derivative document, you fully understand what is written in the original" (Dzhangirov, 2020, 11:06–11:25).

Furthermore, as Dzhangirov noted, the transition of power from Poroshenko to Zelensky was legitimate: "nobody disavowed anyone; nobody canceled anything" (Dzhangirov, 2020, 12:23–12:29). Therefore, what was expected from Ukraine was continuity in its understanding of the Minsk agreements (Dzhangirov, 2020, 12:29–12:38). If Ukraine wanted to refuse to implement the agreement, Dzhangirov argued, it should look for possible ways of renouncing the treaty, such as submitting it for ratification to the parliament:

> Well, there are ways to do this. We do not discuss now if they are right or wrong. But there are acts of manifesting political will. And there are acts of political weakness: "Tell us what is written there, and how we should understand; then, we will decide on whether to fulfill it or not." But, you know, ignorance of the law is no excuse.

Misunderstanding a contract does not exempt one from the need either to fulfill its terms or refuse to do so, Dzhangirov claimed (Dzhangirov, 2020, 12:38–13:30).

The biggest problem of the whole situation, according to Dzhangirov, was that "the president does not understand what he is signing" (Dzhangirov, 2020, 16:51–16:54). It was Zelensky's incompetence in managing the state, in Dzhangirov's view, that created a situation in which those surrounding the president were not capable of advising him well:

> Where can Zelensky get experts if he cannot understand whether a person is an expert or not, if this person acts for good or for bad—both for the country and for him? If you are not competent, where and how can you pick up competent ministers, advisers, and confidants?
>
> (Dzhangirov, 2020, 17:03–17:34)

Interestingly, Dzhangirov confessed that he himself had voted for Zelensky in the second round of the presidential election because he "wanted something different" and because "Poroshenko could no longer be tolerated" (Dzhangirov, 2020, 17:50–18:02). It was the people's choice, Dzhangirov admitted; Ukrainians wanted change, and they believed in the comedian. "Well, we got him," he concluded sadly (Dzhangirov, 2020, 18:02–18:03).

From February 24 to March 8 (the day of his arrest), only two regular videos by Dzhangirov were uploaded to YouTube (the third one was recorded under duress—see below). In one of his regular videos, he discussed what he saw as the two main reasons why the war had started: first, because "on the other side of the border . . . they concluded that Zelensky would not comply with the Minsk agreements under any circumstances" (Dzhangirov, 2022a, 1:05–11:24) and second, because "the West and Zelensky did not want to abandon publicly this [NATO] course for Ukraine" (Dzhangirov, 2022a, 47:14–47:26). In Dzhangirov's view, the West was enabling war within the territory of Ukraine for the purpose of weakening Russia. As for the well-being and lives of Ukrainians, Dzhangirov said, "Let's not feed illusions—they don't care about this at all" (2022b, 29:10–29:13). The cost of the war would be millions of Ukrainian lives, he claimed.

Dzhangirov was highly skeptical regarding the possibility of a peaceful solution to the conflict through negotiation. First, he did not believe in the professionalism of Zelensky's team, whose members—as Dzhangirov (2022a) put it—were "experienced neither in diplomacy nor in public administration" (40:22–40:28). Second, he did not expect Russia to make a deal with Zelensky after the Ukrainian president demonstrated his inability to fulfill his obligations under the Minsk agreements (Dzhangirov, 2022a, 33:30–33:56). Finally, according to Dzhangirov, even if Zelensky and Russia decided to make a peace deal, there would be no mechanism to implement such an agreement, since it would be vehemently opposed by Ukrainian nationalists.

In the last video featuring Dzhangirov (2022c), which was uploaded to YouTube on March 8, 2022, he was dressed in an old sport suit and cap, and he sat limply on a sofa while slowly, in a forlorn voice, condemning

Russia for the invasion. For regular viewers, it was clear that he was speaking under duress (Tkachev, 2022a). As Tkachev commented regarding the video, "Recently, many Kyiv political analysts and bloggers have had the opportunity to participate in such recordings" (Tkachev, 2022b). No news about Dzhangirov has been heard since that day, and it is unclear if he is free or even alive. But what is completely clear is that Dzhangirov's concerns over Zelensky taking the "strange position that everything will sort itself out on its own, even positively" (Dzhangirov, 2020, 15:07–15:17) turned out to be fully justified.

As is evident from the excerpts provided, Dzhangirov—like Buzina, Montyan, and Vasilets—linked the ongoing war in Ukraine to external control over its political decisions, as well as the West's intention of bringing Ukraine into NATO and weakening Russia. Similar to Kotsaba, Sharij, and Tkachev, Dzhangirov also related the tragic outbreak of war in Ukraine to internal factors such as the incompetence, unprofessionalism, and amorality of the Ukrainian government and the ultra-nationalism that has played a decisive role in policy-setting since 2014. Like Kotsaba, Sharij, and Tkachev, Dzhangirov did not welcome the war; this, however, turned out not to be enough to avoid repression.

Epilogue

On February 9, 2022, less than two weeks before Russian troops crossed the border of Ukraine. Its Minister of Foreign Affairs Dmytro Kuleba announced that Ukraine would not comply with the Minsk agreements on the terms put forward by Russia. "This does not mean that we will not implement the Minsk agreements in principle," he said, "but we will not implement them on Russian terms, in the Russian interpretation, in particular through direct dialogue with the DPR and LPR, which Russia categorically insists on, we will not, this is our principled position" (Interfax-Ukraine, 2022). The trouble with this "principled position," however, as explained earlier, was that "Russian terms" were spelled out in Minsk II and the Steinmeier Formula—documents signed by Ukraine, as represented by its presidents, and adopted by international institutions such as the United Nations and OSCE.

Several days after Kuleba's announcement, Putin (2022) made his address to the nation. "We see that the ruling Kyiv elites never stop publicly making clear their unwillingness to comply with the Minsk Package of Measures to settle the conflict and are not interested in a peaceful settlement," he claimed. Arguing for the immediate recognition of the independence and sovereignty of the DPR and LPR, Putin described "the killing of civilians, the blockade, the abuse of people, including children, women and the elderly" (Putin, 2022) that had been taking place in Donbas for the previous eight years, during which time Ukraine was evading its obligation to implement the Minsk agreements. Three days after Putin's address to the nation, Russia attacked Ukraine, cutting the Gordian knot of the agreement that was "impossible to fulfill," in the words of Leonid Kravchuk, the first president of Ukraine (UNIAN, 2020). This was the beginning of a full-scale war and another round of the Ukrainian tragedy that started with the victory of the Euromaidan.

Notes

1 On August 8, 2020, the Central Election Commission of Ukraine decided that no local elections would be held in the 18 districts of the Donetsk and Luhansk regions that were under Kyiv's control (OSCE, 2020, p. 4), depriving half a million Ukrainian citizens of their voting rights for being from the "wrong" territories.
2 I have known Dmitry Dzhangirov since 2002, when I started working as an editor in Kyiv.

Reference List

Allan, D. (2020, May 22). The Minsk conundrum: Western policy and Russia's war in eastern Ukraine. *Chatham House*. www.chathamhouse.org/2020/05/minsk-conundrum-western-policy-and-russias-war-eastern-ukraine-0/minsk-2-agreement

Apukhtin, Y. (2020, August 24). How the Ilovaisk cauldron transformed into the Minsk Agreements. *VK*. https://vk.com/@dnepr_novorossia-kak-ilovaiskii-kotel-transformirovalsya-v-minskie-soglasheni

BBC. (2015, February 7). *Ukraine crisis: 'Last chance' for peace says Hollande*. www.bbc.com/news/world-europe-31185027

BBC. (2019, October 1). *Ukraine agreed to the "Steinmeier formula"* (in Russian). www.bbc.com/russian/news-49898099

Cohen, M., & Green, M. (2016). Ukraine's volunteer battalions. *Center for European Policy Studies*. www.ceps.eu/about-ceps/

Dzhangirov, D. (2020, July 24). Zelensky vs. the Minsk agreements (in Russian). *YouTube*. www.youtube.com/watch?v=Kjxf7nZe4ZQ

Dzhangirov, D. (2022a). Ukraine: What's next? (in Russian). *YouTube*. www.youtube.com/watch?v=m29dhoz3aOo

Dzhangirov, D. (2022b). A new iron curtain descends on us (in Russian). *YouTube*. www.youtube.com/watch?v=cAhllhwnvOo&t=18s

Dzhangirov, D. (2022c). No war! (in Russian). *YouTube*. www.youtube.com/watch?v=_ZLkXarEK9M

Interfax-Ukraine. (2014, December 18). *Putin says that Russians fighting in Donbas act "at the call of the heart," therefore they are not mercenaries* (in Russian). https://ru.interfax.com.ua/news/general/240544.html

Interfax-Ukraine. (2022, February 9). *Kuleba: Macron does not persuade Ukraine to implement Minsk agreements on Russian terms*. https://en.interfax.com.ua/news/general/797207.html

Kostanyan, H., & Meister, S. (2016, June 9). Ukraine, Russia and the EU: Breaking the deadlock in the Minsk process. *Center of European Policy Studies*. www.ceps.eu/ceps-publications/ukraine-russia-and-eu-breaking-deadlock-minsk-process/

Kramer, A. (2015, February 1). Rebels set sights on small eastern Ukraine town. *New York Times*. www.nytimes.com/2015/02/02/world/rebels-set-sights-on-small-eastern-ukraine-town.html?_r=0

Lynch, J. (2019, October 6). Zelensky flounders in bid to end Ukraine's war. *Foreign Policy*. https://foreignpolicy.com/2019/10/11/zelensky-pushes-peace-deal-ukraine-war-russia-Donbas-steinmeier-formula/

Melnikov, R. (2022, October 22). Fights without rules. Lawyer Tatyana Montyan spoke about the special operation and life in Donetsk (in Russian). *RGRU*. https://rg.ru/2022/10/22/boi-bez-pravil-advokat-tatiana-montian-rasskazala-ob-svo-i-zhizni-v-donecke.html

Montyan, T. (2022a, February 19). Scandal in the UN Security Council. War in Ukraine. Speech by Tatyana Montyan (in Russian). *YouTube*. www.youtube.com/watch?v=V9Ds_UZ8Ifs

Montyan, T. (2022b, March 8, 22:40). Dzhango is hostage (in Russian). *Telegram*. t.me/montyan2/118

Myrolub, S. (2022, March 19). Kyiv's unobserved war against dissident public intellectuals. *New Cold War*. https://newcoldwar.org/kyivs-unobserved-war-against-dissident-public-intellectuals/?fbclid=IwAR1LHpSOzu2V6gvucgJQ5g5OkRF_TY_iSXZz0O8haMAidWLak3rCB0WA9V8&mibextid=ATveJy

Nardelli, A. (2021, May 12). EU says Russia is aiming to 'de facto integrate' Eastern Ukraine. *Bloomberg*. www.bloomberg.com/news/articles/2021-05-12/eu-says-russia-is-aiming-to-de-facto-integrate-eastern-ukraine

Newsroom. (2022, December 13). Merkel's confession could be a pretext for an international tribunal. *Modern Diplomacy*. https://moderndiplomacy.eu/2022/12/13/merkels-confession-could-be-a-pretext-for-an-international-tribunal/

OSCE. (2015, February 12). *OSCE chairperson-in-office gives full backing to Minsk package*. www.osce.org/cio/140196

OSCE. (2020). *ODIHR limited election observation mission*. www.osce.org/files/f/documents/e/4/468249.pdf

Poroshenko, P. (2015, September 11). I will not negotiate with militants and terrorists (in Ukrainian). *Interfax-Ukraine*. https://interfax.com.ua/news/political/289446.html

Poroshenko, P. (2022, June 15). Poroshenko on Minsk agreements (in Ukrainian). *European Solidarity*. https://eurosolidarity.org/2022/06/15/poroshenko-pro-minski-domovlenosti-my-otrymaly-visim-rokiv-shhob-stvoryty-zsu-i-vidnovyty-ekonomiku

President of Ukraine. (2019, December 9). *Overall agreed conclusions of the Paris summit in the Normandy format of December 9, 2019*. www.president.gov.ua/en/news/zagalni-uzgodzheni-visnovki-parizkogo-samitu-v-normandskomu-58797

President of Ukraine. (2020, July 23). *Agreement on a full and comprehensive ceasefire on the demarcation line in Donbas awaits signing by all parties of the Normandy format* (in Ukrainian). www.president.gov.ua/news/volodimir-zelenskij-ugoda-pro-povne-ta-vseosyazhne-pripinenn-62409

Protocol. (2014, September 5). *Peace agreements database*. www.peaceagreements.org/viewmasterdocument/1363

Prouvost, T. (2022, December 28). Hollande: "There will only be a way out of the conflict when Russia fails on the ground." *Kyiv Independent*. https://kyivindependent.com/national/hollande-there-will-only-be-a-way-out-of-the-conflict-when-russia-fails-on-the-ground

Putin, V. (2014, August 29). Russian President Vladimir Putin addressed the militia of Novorossiya (in Russian). *President of Russia*. www.kremlin.ru/events/president/news/46506

Putin, V. (2022, February 21). Address by the President of the Russian Federation. *Kremlin.* http://en.kremlin.ru/events/president/news/67828

Roshchina, O. (2023, February 9). Minsk agreements were simple way to end war by ceding territories to Russia. *Ukrainska Pravda.* www.pravda.com.ua/eng/news/2023/02/9/7388717/

Shramovych, V. (2019, August 29). "I'm still in Ilovaisk": Memories of August 2014 (in Russian). *BBC.* www.bbc.com/ukrainian/features-russian-49486774

Soldatkin, V., & Polityuk, P. (2015, February 12). "Glimmer of hope" for Ukraine after new ceasefire deal. *Reuters.* www.reuters.com/article/us-ukraine-crisis-idUSKB N0LG0FX20150212

Tkachev, Y. (2022a, March 3). The monstrous aftermath of an airstrike (in Russian). *Telegram.* https://t.me/dadzibao/6069

Tkachev, Y. (2022b, March 8). I think you have already seen the SSU video (in Russian). *Telegram.* https://t.me/dadzibao/6454

Tucker, M. (2015a, January 20). Kremlin-backed separatists rain death down on Debaltseve. *Kyiv Post.* www.kyivpost.com/article/content/war-against-ukraine/kremlin-backed-separatists-rain-death-down-on-debaltseve-377923.html

Tucker, M. (2015b, February 3). Kremlin-backed separatists look to level Debaltseve. *Kyiv Post.* www.kyivpost.com/article/content/war-against-ukraine/kremlin-backed-separatists-look-to-level-debaltseve-379386.html

UN. (2015, February 17). *Unanimously adopting resolution 2202 (2015), Security Council calls on parties to implement accords aimed at peaceful settlement in Eastern Ukraine.* www.un.org/press/en/2015/sc11785.doc.htm

UNIAN. (2015, February 12). *Minsk agreement: Full text in English.* www.unian.info/politics/1043394-minsk-agreement-full-text-in-english.html

UNIAN. (2020, September 11). *Minsk agreements impossible to fulfill–Ukraine's Kravchuk.* www.unian.info/politics/donbas-war-minsk-agreements-impossible-to-fulfill-kravchuk-says-11144114.html

Zelensky, V. (2022a, April 7). President Volodymyr Zelenskyy gave an interview to the Indian mass media republic media network (in Ukrainian). *YouTube.* www.youtube.com/watch?v=25m3OnNnDRQ

Zelensky, V. (2022b, May 4). Speech by the President of Ukraine Volodymyr Zelensky at the *Wall Street Journal* CEO council summit session (in Ukrainian). *YouTube.* www.youtube.com/watch?v=SxskLGTvbPE

Zelensky, V. (2022c, May 13). Negotiations with the Russian federation, Italy as a mediator, evacuation of the wounded from "Azovstal." Zelensky's interview (in Ukrainian). *YouTube.* www.youtube.com/watch?v=W8rQf75GMUg

Zelensky, V. (2022d, July 28). Full interview with Piers Morgan. *YouTube.* www.youtube.com/watch?v=hGnZWcazZas

Zelensky, V. (2022e, August 29). Zelensky turned to the participants of the strategic forum in Slovenian Bled (in Ukrainian). *YouTube.* www.youtube.com/watch?v=a23K-WJg6Go

Zelensky, V. (2022f, September 12). Zelensky's interview with Farid Zakaria for CNN (in Ukrainian). *YouTube.* www.youtube.com/watch?v=pq6RwJ3AqO8

Zinets, N., & Dyomkin, D. (2015, January 26). Ukraine rebels move to encircle government troops in new advance. *Reuters.* www.reuters.com/article/us-ukraine-crisis-military-idUSKBN0KZ0L920150126

Conclusion. A Road to Peace
Giving Voice to the Silenced

Ukrainian President Volodymyr Zelensky's articulations of the war with Russia, presented in this book, can serve as a good illustration of Ernesto Laclau's theory of populism, which explains the logic behind the discursive construction of a unified collective of "good people"—the essence of any populist project. As discussed in Chapter 2, the simplification of the social to the extreme and its Manichean division into a clear dichotomy of "us" versus "them" are the most distinguishable features of populism. This enterprise, described by Laclau as "impossible and necessary," stems from the structural need to enact discursive closure in an effort to define the boundaries of a populist collective and exclude "others." For Zelensky, creating a populist global totality of "civilized" people has also been both impossible and necessary. It is impossible to reduce into a simple dichotomy the broad and highly complex sociopolitical landscape that Zelensky has been trying to hegemonize, but it is a necessary effort in his populist project, because only through discursive closure can he appeal to his discursively created transnational community of "civilized people." As my analysis in Chapter 3 shows, Zelensky has been constructing this imagined transnational community in strictly populist terms, ignoring the internal diversity of the sociopolitical landscape he wanted to hegemonize for his political purposes.

This discursive closure required naming, and the name of Zelensky—specifically, the discursive-material assemblage represented by his name (the unity of his body, voice, gestures, facial expressions, military-style clothing, and so on)—has been essential in assembling heterogeneous elements into the newly established totality of a "civilized" collective. Once the equivalential chain of his transnational publics became so wide—encompassing the states of North America, Europe, Africa, Asia, and Australia—the vagueness of Zelensky's language about the conflict also became a structural necessity. That is why his definitions have been so imprecise and fluctuating, while his narrative of the situation is full of mythical imagery about barbarians fighting against civilized people, democratic Ukraine against autocratic Russia, the modern forces of today against the outdated forces of the past, the united good versus total evil, and so forth. The fact that Zelensky has never discussed

DOI: 10.4324/9781003379164-10

the actual disunity of Ukraine with his global audiences while only resorting to this theme among Ukrainian journalists clearly points to the "calculated ambivalence" (Wodak & Forchtner, 2014, p. 14) of his interviews and speeches intended for foreigners.

In line with Laclau's argument that the process of hegemonic investment of one element (in this case, Zelensky) with the mythical fullness of the whole populist collective (the civilized world) is unthinkable without affect, Zelensky's performances have appealed to the emotions of his audiences (Dyczok & Chung, 2022). His passionate speeches have been punctuated by frequent hand gestures such as banging his fist on the table and placing his hand over his heart (Zelensky, 2022e, 13:50–14:15). He showed his transnational audiences videos of Ukraine's suffering under Russian bombs (Zelensky, 2022d, 13:16–15:50), confessed to journalists about "feeling pain" (Zelensky, 2022j, 6:43–46:44) and having "only one emotion—hate" (Zelensky, 2022p, 28:08–28:10), and called Russians "non-humans" [нелюди] (Zelensky, 2022b, 4:37), "monsters" [потвори] (Zelensky, 2022c, 3:40), "butchers" [кати] (Zelensky, 2022g, 9:34–39:35), "bastards" [скоти] (Zelensky, 2022o, 3:21), and so forth.

In his speeches, Zelensky systematically highlighted claims of Russian atrocities, telling of "mass deportations" (Zelensky, 2022g, 2:21–22:22), "hundreds of cases of rape," including "small children and even babies" (2022f, 3:01–3:14), and "mobile crematoria—machines for destroying human bodies" that Russians, according to Zelensky, used "to hide the traces of war crimes" (Zelensky, 2022h, 8:02–8:18). Zelensky needed these stories—whether true or not[1]—to achieve affect, without which, as Laclau (2005) argues, no populist project can come into being.

With the passionate formulation of Zelensky's "popular demand" of the "civilized world" in the fight against "barbarians," an antagonistic frontier separating good from evil emerged; the global social came to be dichotomized. This dichotomization required not only an affective investment but also the elimination from the public view of any media presentations with more comprehensive information on the war's atrocities, presenting those committed by Russians as well as by Ukrainians: "cases of torture and ill-treatment" (UN OHCHR, 2022) or the usage of banned landmines "causing civilian casualties" (Human Rights Watch, 2023). That is why it was so important for Zelensky to shut down all the discursive-material assemblages of opposition voices leaning toward alternative or simply balanced depictions of what was going on.

Despite the fact that Zelensky's equivalential chain has been extended to the extreme and in this sense can be called "inclusive," in practice this "inclusivity" has only been superficial. What has remained hidden from public view (especially for global publics lacking adequate knowledge of the nuances of the Ukraine situation) is the mechanism for achieving this "inclusivity"/"extension": the elimination from the field of political representation all oppositional voices seeking to destabilize Zelensky's totalitarian closures. Structurally speaking, this seems to be one of the biggest problems of populism, which prescribes the annihilation (symbolic or not) of "otherness" that does not fit into the rosy picture of "good people" united to confront evil.

Unlike the populists of the Euromaidan, who explicitly argued that some groups of people are "unworthy" ("slaves," "vatniki," and "sovki"), Zelensky does not exclude cultural "others" openly. He veils this exclusion with the discourse of unity, making internal splits invisible; only "collaborators"/"traitors" are excluded from the ranks of "united Ukrainians." By definition, however, "collaborators" cannot be considered the representatives of sociocultural groups whose opinions deserve attention, and "traitors" in Zelensky's presentations are always individuals who undermine the national security of Ukraine and thus violate its criminal code. It is as a result of this strategic "suturing" of Ukraine into an impossible social totality (Laclau & Mouffe, 1985, p. 107) that all people holding alternative views came to be seen as criminals whose outlooks should not be considered. Since the Euromaidan, Ukraine's border regions—neither purely Ukrainian nor entirely Russian—have been suffering the most from this "suturing" of the social. The population of these regions has been annihilated, first symbolically, through discursive othering (see Chapter 1), and later physically, as the hostilities of Ukraine's ATO and Russia's SMO have been taking place in these areas. This is the tragedy, tracing its origins to the Euromaidan, that has overtaken the southeast of Ukraine.

As Laclau (2005) argues, the difference between institutionalism and populism is that the former constructs the social by the logic of difference, which does not presuppose an antagonistic frontier, while the latter uses the logic of equivalence, which cannot be performed without the antagonistic dichotomization of the social. It is here that we observe the democratic discursive closure of which Mouffe (2009) warns. By suppressing differences in the name of unity, populism may create irreconcilable antagonisms if the frontier between "us" and "them" is presented not as unstable, contingent, and temporary, but as essential, natural, and immutable.

The central feature of Zelensky's populist discourse is its radical antagonization of the social. By articulating Russia as uncivilized, barbaric, and tyrannical, while depicting Ukraine (as part of the civilized world) as civilized, free, and democratic, Zelensky has established the distance between the two as dramatic and insurmountable. "[Russia] is thousands of light years away from us, from normal people," Zelensky (2022a) argued (March 4, 6:12–16:18). Similarly, while presenting Ukraine as a coherent whole with "one thought, one friend, and one enemy" (Zelensky, 2022i, 22:46–22:51) and calling oppositional voices "collaborators," "traitors," and "fake journalists who carry lies" (Zelensky, 2022m, 51:18–51:21), Zelensky established the "otherness" of the latter as persistent and irreversible.

No negotiations, either in the first case (with Russia) or in the second (with the opposition), have been prescribed in this Manichean division of the social endorsed by Zelensky. "It is very important that there are no gray zones," he claimed (Zelensky, 2022k, 53:52–53:54), although it is precisely in "gray areas" that differences are usually negotiated and compromises are reached. In this light, it only makes sense that Zelensky would openly devalue diplomacy with the argument that "the truth is faster than lies and than diplomacy" (Zelensky, 2022s, 12:48–12:54).

In line with Carpentier's (2017) conceptualization of antagonistic discourse, which is characterized by the hierarchical presentation of the superior self and the inferior other, Zelensky has been positioning Russia, with all its citizens, at the lowest point on the civilizational scale of development: "The time of such countries and rulers has passed. And our time is our time. This is the future" (Zelensky, 2022l, 9:00–9:10); "a nuclear state [of Russia] that is stuck in the past" (Zelensky, 2022n, 1:54–61:57); and so forth. This presentation of Russia is reminiscent of the dominant discourse of post-Maidan Ukraine, in which both Russians and Ukraine's Russophones appear as underdeveloped creatures who "live in a time that is behind our contemporality by at least 20 years" (Zvinyatskivska, 2014). While articulating Ukraine as a unified social body from which only malignant tumors—traitors and collaborators—are excised, Zelensky homogenized both the self and the other, ignoring all the complexity of the social and the nuances of oppositional opinions.

Mouffe (2009) warns that the stabilization of closures through the establishment of solid dividing frontiers leads to totalitarian tendencies in governance and provokes various antagonisms; the case of Zelensky illustrates both the former and the latter. Instead of seeing oppositional journalists and bloggers as adversaries who want to organize the common symbolic space in a different way, Zelensky's regime has been presenting them as enemies and prosecuting them as such. In a similar fashion, instead of seeing foreign leaders who adopt a neutral stance as trying to preserve the symbolic space necessary for negotiations and diplomatic solutions, Zelensky has been accusing them of playing along with evil. "I believe that there can be no neutrality in the matter of good and evil," he claimed (Zelensky, 2022q, 1:32–41:37). This is the logical outcome of his civilizational populism: With Russia presented as "total evil" and the deadly enemy of human civilization, no compromise can be viewed as acceptable. The story of Armageddon propagated by Zelensky, which presupposes fighting until the bitter end, puts compromise beyond the limits of the thinkable, making it an inconceivable option.

From Antagonism to Agonism

As mentioned in the introductory part of this book, the question of whether transnational populism contributes to a more conflictual character of international relations was central to my research. My findings suggest that the answer to this question may be positive. Structurally speaking, the necessity of forming broad populist fronts requires not only ignoring all nuances and contradictions but also pathologizing those who insist on taking the complexities into account. Since the presentation of such deviating "others" as enemies of the people in need of eradication/punishment/silencing appears to be a structural necessity, any populist project seems inherently antagonistic. This antagonism may not take on a radical authoritarian form if populist leaders are sophisticated enough to realize that managing large collectives of people requires complex strategies for dealing with both particularistic and equivalential logics, though such a case was not considered in this book.

Of course, it is difficult to expect the leader of a war-torn nation to be fully responsive to the needs of diverse sociocultural groups both within national borders and across them. Any war requires the mobilization of public opinion and creation of a national front against a common enemy, and it would be naïve to expect otherwise. There are two important factors, however, that need to be kept in mind in this respect. First, Zelensky's populist project involving the strict dichotomization of the social started long before the war (see Chapter 1), with the onset of Russia's SMO only reconfiguring his domestic populism into a transnational one. Second, this reconfiguration—from domestic to transnational—could not have happened without powerful global institutions and media platforms hegemonizing the established dichotomy on an unprecedented scale. Critical thinkers have little doubt as to how this global hegemonization of Zelensky's populist discourse has been achieved. As John Hartley (2023) puts it,

> As soon as Putin was identified as the villain, a hero was needed, and was indeed waiting in the wings. When Volodymyr Zelenskyy abandoned his business suit for olive drab fatigues, the stage was set.
>
> (p. 13)

> A 'global' anti-Russian alliance was assembled to reinforce and extend the USA's 'sphere of influence', while denying Russia's claim to its own. . . . The alliance may have involved multiple countries, but the narrative belonged only to one.
>
> (p. 14)

This is because the strategic construction of narratives is crucial in geopolitical struggles, as John Arquilla and David Ronfeldt (1999), the architects of the RAND Corporation's "noosphere" policy initiative, acknowledged as early as the turn of the millennium.

If global media and other neoliberal institutions that have been providing Zelensky with an opportunity to reach global audiences had kept an analytical balance and abstained from the radical dichotomization of the social, a symbolic space necessary for communication, negotiation, and compromise would have been preserved. This has not happened, however, due to the geopolitical interests of various global players. What humanity is left with as a result is a "maximum separation," to put it in Laclau and Mouffe's terms, where "two societies" appear in place of one, and the confrontation between these "societies" becomes "fierce, total and indiscriminate: there exist no discourses capable of establishing differences within an equivalential chain in which each and every one of its elements symbolizes evil" (Laclau & Mouffe, 1985, p. 129).

If projected onto the global geopolitical stage, this "maximum separation" implies a "fierce, total, and indiscriminate" fight between two irreconcilable parts of the world—"civilizational good" and "barbarian evil." This is exactly what Zelensky and the global institutions of power closing his discourse on a global scale drive at: a zero-sum game, an ultimate battle until one side falls. In the age of modern weaponry, this dangerous fantasy, based on the implausible premise that one side of the conflict is morally pure while the other is not, may put everyone on the planet at risk.

To disrupt these lethal dynamics, antagonism needs to be transformed into agonism through the rearticulation of the nodal points of antagonistic discourse and recreation of a common symbolic space necessary for a political/diplomatic process. To re-establish "conflictual togetherness," as Carpentier (2017, p. 178) puts it, a structural balance needs to be restored so that the involved actors are no longer positioned hierarchically. It is also necessary to move away from dichotomization, making the solid, impermeable frontiers between opponents more porous, in order to activate a diversity of positions and allow pluralism to flourish—a precondition for agonism to emerge.

This transformation of antagonism into agonism enables recognition that there are legitimate concerns on each side of the divide. Alternatively, the continued prosecution and silencing of "others" by the forces of "good" not only erodes independence of thought, as Orwell admonished, but also the prospects for lasting peace and the likelihood of avoiding a nuclear Armageddon. When authoritarian populism goes abroad with its ultra-simplified antagonistic judgment, and its views are then hegemonized worldwide by global media and other powerful institutions, the specter of such a final war comes closer to reality. Zelensky's call to take preemptive action against Russia (Zelensky, 2022r, 25:16–26:00), which many interpreted as a call for a preemptive nuclear strike (e.g., Call, 2022), can be seen as an illustration of the massive global risk of simplistic judgment.

Restoring the complexity of intellectual judgment is not the same as restoring the Russian empire/tyranny/barbarism, as authoritarian populists want us to believe; taking into consideration oppositional arguments is not the same as promoting the Kremlin's agenda. As my analysis of the oppositional discourse of Ukrainian journalists and bloggers presented in this book suggests, independent critical judgment—non-imperial, non-tyrannical, and non-barbaric—is also possible. It exists even though it is being hidden from the view of broad publics. It is this excluded critical judgment that enables recognition of the floating character of all the nodal points of Zelensky's discourse: The

Euromaidan may be seen as both "the revolution of dignity" and a "coup d'état"; the Donbas uprising as both "terrorism" and a "fight for freedom"; the ATO as both a "civil war" and a "Russian invasion"; the non-implementation of the Minsk agreements as both Russia's and Ukraine's fault; Ukrainian dissidents as both "oppositionists" and "traitors"; and so on. If the floating nature of discursively constructed reality is acknowledged, global publics will come to a far more sophisticated and nuanced understanding of global conflicts. This, in turn, will invite the formulation of alternative visions and initiatives for peace. Peace can hardly be achieved without respect for complexity and a willingness to compromise, two areas in which populism is sorely lacking.

Note

1 No independent reporting has proven the existence of mobile crematoria used by Russia (Creedon, 2022). Meanwhile, it is a proven fact that many stories about children being raped by the Russian military were invented by Ukraine's ex-Ombudsman Lyudmila Denisova, who was fired for these fabrications in June 2022 (Lukasheva, 2022).

Reference List

Arquilla, J., & Ronfeldt, R. (1999). *The emergence of noopolitik: Toward an American information strategy.* RAND Corporation. www.rand.org/content/dam/rand/pubs/monograph_reports/MR1033/RAND_MR1 033.pdf

Call, B. (2022, October 7). Fact check: Did President Zelensky call on NATO to start nuclear war? *Newsweek.* www.newsweek.com/zelensky-nuclear-putin-russia-war-pre-emptive-1749781

Carpentier, N. (2017). *The discursive-material knot: Cyprus in conflict and community media participation.* Peter Lang.

Creedon, J. (2022, April 13). Fake images of Russian "mobile crematorium" in Ukraine. *France 24.* www.france24.com/en/tv-shows/truth-or-fake/20220413-fake-images-of-russian-mobile-crematorium-in-ukraine

Dyczok, M., & Chung, Y. (2022). Zelens'kyi uses his communication skills as a weapon of war. *Canadian Slavonic Papers, 64*(2–3), 146–161. doi:10.1080/00085006.2022.2106699

Hartley, J. (2023). Strategic stories: Weaponized or worldmaking? *Global Media and China.* Online before print. doi:10.1177/20594364231153200

Human Rights Watch. (2023, January 31). *Banned landmines harm civilians.* www.hrw.org/news/2023/01/31/ukraine-banned-landmines-harm-civilians

Laclau, E. (2005). *On populist reason.* Verso.

Laclau, E., & Mouffe, C. (1985). *Hegemony and socialist strategy: Towards a radical democratic politics.* Verso.

Lukasheva, S. (2022, June 27). From Facebook to interrogations. Why did ombudsman Denisova lose her position (in Ukrainian). *Ukrainska Pravda.* www.pravda.com.ua/articles/2022/06/27/7354838/

Mouffe, C. (2009). *The democratic paradox.* Verso.

UN OHCHR. (2022, November 15). *Ukraine/Russia: Prisoners of war*. Office of the United Nations High Commissioner for Human Rights. www.ohchr.org/en/press-briefing-notes/2022/11/ukraine-russia-prisoners-war

Wodak, R., & Forchtner, B. (2014). Embattled Vienna 1683/2010: Right-wing populism, collective memory and the fictionalisation of politics. *Visual Communication, 13*(2), 231–255. doi:10.1177/147 0357213516720

Zelensky, V. (2022a, March 4). We experienced a night that could stop the history of Ukraine and Europe (in Ukrainian). *YouTube*. www.youtube.com/watch?v=qQ_4QpEftp8

Zelensky, V. (2022b, March 8). 12th day of the war. Evening address of the President of Ukraine Volodymyr Zelensky to Ukrainians (in Ukrainian). *YouTube*. www.youtube.com/watch?v=t3f3vzpJOeQ

Zelensky, V. (2022c, March 10). 15th day of the war. Evening address of the President of Ukraine Volodymyr Zelensky to Ukrainians (in Ukrainian). *YouTube*. www.youtube.com/watch?v=_8M8_a6cxZ4

Zelensky, V. (2022d, March 16). Volodymyr Zelensky spoke before the US Congress (in Ukrainian). *YouTube*. www.youtube.com/watch?v=HILlSCcphUc

Zelensky, V. (2022e, April 5). Volodymyr Zelensky addressed high-ranking officials and members of the UN Security Council (in Ukrainian). *YouTube*. www.youtube.com/watch?v=Hvu6MUh0hco

Zelensky, V. (2022f, April 12). Volodymyr Zelensky addressed the people and politicians of Lithuania (in Ukrainian). *YouTube*. www.youtube.com/watch?v=6Fo-o2s6nqk

Zelensky, V. (2022g, April 13). Volodymyr Zelensky addressed the people and politicians of Estonia (in Ukrainian). *YouTube*. www.youtube.com/watch?v=yPAh-PlJmiA

Zelensky, V. (2022h, April 21). To the Portuguese. Address of the President of Ukraine Volodymyr Zelensky (in Ukrainian). *YouTube*. www.youtube.com/watch?v=fjfe 7XnglkE

Zelensky, V. (2022i, April 29). Volodymyr Zelensky spoke with representatives of the Polish mass media (in Ukrainian). *YouTube*. www.youtube.com/watch?v=uobFhTgr96k

Zelensky, V. (2022j, May 2). Volodymyr Zelensky's interview for the 60 Minutes project of the Australian television channel Nine Network (in Ukrainian). *YouTube*. www.youtube.com/watch?v=iRtp89_ZspA

Zelensky, V. (2022k, May 11). *Volodymyr Zelensky talked with students of leading French Universities* (in Ukrainian). www.youtube.com/watch?v=gV_w5QFrnpA

Zelensky, V. (2022l, June 10). Communication of Volodymyr Zelensky with students and professors of educational institutions of Great Britain (in Ukrainian). *YouTube*. www.youtube.com/watch?v=pyRXw_cxhxU

Zelensky, V. (2022m, June 14). *Zelensky gave an online press conference for representatives of Danish ZMI* (in Ukrainian). www.youtube.com/watch?v=7e0X_FQPpXo

Zelensky, V. (2022n, June 21). Zelensky's address to the participants of the Cannes Lions international festival of creativity (in Ukrainian). *YouTube*. www.youtube.com/watch?v=ATQ95CCuGR4

Zelensky, V. (2022o, July 14). Zelensky addressed the participants of the conference in The Hague regarding the responsibility of the Russian Federation for crimes in Ukraine (in Ukrainian). *YouTube*. www.youtube.com/watch?v=_Jhhg42-eMs

Zelensky, V. (2022p, July 28). Zelensky's full interview with Piers Morgan (in Ukrainian). *YouTube*. www.youtube.com/watch?v=hGnZWcazZas

Zelensky, V. (2022q, September 30). Zelensky's communication with the University of Zurich community, business and cantonal authorities (in Ukrainian). *YouTube*. www.youtube.com/watch?v=O1l_ZEICaDY

Zelensky, V. (2022r, October 6). A special address by Volodymyr Zelensky, President of Ukraine. *Lowy Institute*. www.lowyinstitute.org/event/special-address-volodymyr-zelenskyy-president-ukraine

Zelensky, V. (2022s, October 13). Zelensky gave an interview to the German public broadcaster ZDF (in Ukrainian). *YouTube*. www.youtube.com/watch?v=PQiYjg26gKU

Zvinyatskivska, Zoya. (2014, February 6). The war of times, or 20 years that we have lost (in Ukrainian). *Ukrainska Pravda*. http://life.pravda.com.ua/columns/2014/02/6/151566/

Index

For Product Safety Concerns and Information please contact our EU
representative GPSR@taylorandfrancis.com
Taylor & Francis Verlag GmbH, Kaufingerstraße 24, 80331 München, Germany